MULTIVERSE

MULTIVERSE

POEMS BY

JONEL ABELLANOSA

Clare Songbirds
Publishing House

Poems by Jonel Abellanosa
Clare Songbirds Publishing House Poetry Series
ISBN 978-1-947653-57-3
Clare Songbirds Publishing House
Multiverse © 2019 Jonel Abellanosa

Printed in the United States of America
FIRST EDITION

Clare Songbirds Publishing House
Auburn, New York 13021
www.claresongbirdspub.com

For Dexter, Nicola and Donna

The author wishes to thank the following journals where the poems first appeared:

The McNeese Review (McNeese State University, Louisiana): "Ode to the Sun"
Rattle: "To the Red Fire Monkey"
Allegro Poetry Journal (United Kingdom): "Tao of Indoor Walk"
GNU Journal (National University): "Archivist"
Five Willows Literary Journal: "Simplicity," "Interplanetary Caravan"
Carbon Culture Review: "Machine Language"
Poetry Kanto (Kanto Gakuin University, Japan): "Drawing," "Blooms," "Healer," "Empath"
New Mystics: "Science," "Of Another Kind," "Ode to Aloe Vera," "Lazarus," "Higher," "Lament of the Cello's Scroll," "Aubade"
*The Ofi Press (*Mexico): "Manual," "After Midnight"
Philippine Graphic Magazine: "Apple," "The Dancer," "Psyche," "Flash Fiction"
The Indiana Voice Journal: "Card Reading," "Echo"
Yellow Chair Review: "Dexter," "Visitation"
Kind of a Hurricane Press (Barometric Pressures Author Series): "Glossolalia" (from my chapbook *Pictures of the Floating World)*
Otoliths (Australia): "Lunch Break," "Kite"
The Bangalore Review (India): "Ode to the Tree of Life"
Black Poppy Review: "Everlasting Grief"
Dark Matter Literary Journal (University of Houston, Downtown): "Ode to the Moon," "Mixing Metaphors for Effects"
Windhover Journal (University of Mary Hardin-Baylor): "Man Born Blind"
Ancient Paths Literary Journal: "Simon Peter"
Penwood Review: "Nicodemus," "According to the Leaves"
Golden Lantern: Poetry in the Essence of Buddhism and Taoism: "Lullaby," "Blueberries"
*Anak Sastra: Stories of Southeast Asia (*Malaysia): "Mahjong," "Flute for His Newborn," "Ode to Green Tea"
*Poetry Pacific (*Canada): "Mahjong," "Visitation"
*Eastlit (*Thailand): "Medium"
Anglican Theological Review: "Boy with Five Loaves and Two Fish"
*Deep Water Literary Journal (*Ireland): "Mozart's Last Words," "Quatrains," "Unchristened"

*Philippine PEN Literary Journal (*Inaugural Issue with the theme *Healing): *"Second Sight"
Dead Snakes: "Mind and Body," "To My Tooth"
The Penmen Review (Southern New Hampshire University): "On the Balcony," "In My View"
PEN Peace Mindanao Anthology (University of Santo Tomas Press): "Mindanao"
Digital Papercut (Wordpool Press): "Fish Vendor," "To the Ants"
Fox Chase Review: "Demolition Job," "The Photographer," "Rehearsal"
*New Verse News (*Indonesia): "Children of the War," "Warning:
Graphic Images Not Suitable for Children," "Convergence"
The Lyric: "2012"
Qarrtsiluni: "Massacre in Maguindanao"
Life is a Rollercoaster Anthology (Kind of a Hurricane Press): "The Guitarist"
The Artistic Muse: "Maya"
Liquid Imagination: "The Soloist"
The Camel Saloon: "One," "Francis of the Poor"
Jellyfish Whispers: "While the Crickets are Mating"
Poetry Quarterly: "Reversing the Alchemy," "The Tempo," "Piano"
Shot Glass Journal: "Top," "The Dance"
Gadfly: Culture that Matters: "Cats on the Roof," "Dexter"
Red River Review: "Echo"
Pyrokinection: "Rhythm," "Igloo Booth," "Breakthrough"
Four Seasons Anthology (Kind of a Hurricane Press): "Thirteen Ways of Looking"
Marsh Hawk Review: "Thirteen Ways of Looking"
Pedestal Magazine: "Jack"
Lontar: The Journal of Southeast Asian Speculative Fiction: "Pinocchio," "Rapunzel"
Mobius Journal of Social Change: "Aliens vs. Predators"
Star*Line (Science Fiction Poetry Association): "Blue Hour," "Cyborg"
Inkscrawl: "Nonfiction"
Dwarf Stars Anthology 2015 (Science Fiction Poetry Association): "Nonfiction"
Inwood Indiana Press: "Man with the Cure," "Dolls"
Eye to the Telescope (Science Fiction Poetry Association): "Transit of Venus"
Barefoot Review: "The Price"
High Coupe: "Before I was Born"

Poetry Superhighway: "To the Ants," "Tablet"
*Cha: An Asian Literary Journal (*Hong Kong): "Pictures of the Floating World"
Night Ballet Press Delirious Prince Tribute Anthology: "Pan"
Millennium Poets and Poems: Birdsong Anthology 2016: "To Light"
The Fifty-Two: Crime Poetry: "Pied Piper"
Spirit Fire Review – "Ode to the Holy Spirit" (nominated for the Pushcart Prize), "Mary of Bethany"
Dissident Voice – "Before and After the Dictator"
The Literary Hatchet – "Lovers in a Fresco," "Vincent's Ear," Doorway"
The Peacock Journal: "Mindspeak," "Otherness," "illusionist," "Teacher," "Juggler"
Immix: The Journal of Social Justice: "Lovers in a Mural"
Episteme Literary Journal (Bharat College, India): "Clues," "Poetics," "Photographer"
The Sourland Mountain Review: "Imagination"
First Literary Review – *East* – "Nightfall," Lovers in a Painting"
Haikuniverse – "Bolt of Lightning"
Setu Magazine – "The River Speaks," "Ode to the Miracle Plant," "Before the Night Journey"
The Bees Are Dead Literary Journal: "Epiphany," "Game of the Elders"
Poppy Road Review – "Our Old House"
The Chicago Record – "Traffic Jam," "Independence Day Celebrations"

CONTENTS

SPIRIT/SPIRITUAL DIMENSION

TERRESTRIAL DIMENSION

ARS POETICA/CREATIVE DIMENSION

EXTRATERRESTRIAL/SPECULATIVE DIMENSION

PERSONAL DIMENSION

PICTURES OF THE FLOATING WORLD

ACROSTIC MULTIVERSE

ODE TO THE SUN

Aphelion, as when I'm away brooding or
Basking, questions like corona. My bones
Crave strength, your morning flares like
Dandelions, neighborhood waking with joggers,
Early sizzling of pans in corner stores. I follow the
Familiar with rubber shoes, circling like my mind's
Gnomon. Running stirs imagination—a
Heliotrope. After an hour of exercises and recalls
I retreat to my room, in shadows, brew
Jasmine tea, in my poetry's woods reshaping
Knots, feel rejuvenation in my veins, your
Light like blood to organs. I invoke your
Melodies, secrets of magnifying life,
Noting how movements turn familiar
Or varied. I often doubt my descriptions like
Partial eclipses, as if unknowns bring me to
Quiet. These moments glow as silks of
Reticence, introversion like books in boxes,
Spaces longing to be ordered. I picture
Transformations in your touches, echo the
Unpurified but also labor for the true in my
Visualizations, trusting your revelations.
Wise bestower, grant me seeing and
Extend my understanding. I dwell in
Your colors, angling this glass to your
Zenith—to filter your tenderest sparkles

TO THE RED FIRE MONKEY

Ama*, papa's mom who loved me more than anyone,
Blamed the year I was born—1968—her ethnic
Chinese biases answering why unruliness ruled our home.
Disciplining me was possible when she's not around,
Every now and then belt coiled round papa's hand. Her
Firstborn, papa's elder brother, tied my wrist to the
Grillwork after I instigated my younger cousin to
Hose the floor with our piss. Uncle must have known
It was a mistake when Ama arrived home. What he did
Jerked the dragon in grandma's heart and she fumed,
Knifing her eldest son's authority with scary scolds. "Your
love for that monkey is spoiling him!" —I remember
My uncle's words as he argued. My grades began to
Nosedive, report cards decorated with red numbers
Of failing marks, papa and mom like patrons of the
Principal's office. Nicknamed "Monkey," I skipped
Quizzes, classes. Forward ten years or so and I was a
Red as shiver junkie smoking for decades, my life like
Siesta hours of childhood that seldom knew silence.
This year, 2016, how many children, born of red and fire,
Unleashing monkey business as homage to you? How
Vicious can playfulness be? Red and Fire seem
Worse enough. Add Monkey to the mix and all
Expectations fly out the window like banana peels,
Your year guaranteed with the funniest brow raisers,
Zaniest behaviors as cure-all for conformists

*Ama is how I addressed my grandmother

Moving, reverential pacing, in minimalist sounds, under an
Incense-colored ceiling, mist like the wind's inverness. The
Numinous slakes like water's lulling murmur. I'm lesser than
Dewdrops on stones, as I circle barefoot on marble. Here,
Shadows home in rituals of summer. My heart dwells with
Chirps from trees older than my grandparents, melodious.
Attuned, I tie ribbons of my gratefulness to the bonsai
Pruned between prayer and the moon's passage,
Each reclaimed step a hymn to solitude

ARCHIVIST

"Afterlife" needs redefinition when this technology
Becomes public. We're pioneers of preserving
Consciousness. First among equals, Jobs, his mind
Downloaded and stored before his brain and body
Expired, the virtual Steve now omnipresent: we've seen
Forms of otherworlds he sees—as presentations of
Gripping colorations, or it's his imagination. Kaleidoscopic
Holograms suggest lilts and lurements of language:
(I thought I saw Einstein and his smazed smile.) My
Job ensures the Visionary Minds database workable,
Keeping snapshots of next realms like abstractions,
Loading the right consciousness for consultations. The
Mind of Steve Jobs has been uploaded dozens of times,
Norms of his thinking for epigenetic algorithms. I
Offset my aloneness manning digital shelves, writing
Poetry as caffeine for boredom. I wonder if my poems are
Quixotic enough to earn me a place next to Heaney and
Rich, their new poems from the beyond haunting my
Sleepiness. Diabetes overrunning my body, taking its
Toll on physicality. Could my work or poems secure the
Understanding that my senses be saved, here?
Vanity. My role doesn't require exotic skills.
When I leave this body I won't want to be summoned by
Expectations. I've neither answers nor achievements, only
Years of perseverance. They want prophecy from poets,
Zones of mind whose accuracies proceed from words

SIMPLICITY

My return to the ordinary, ways of
Each day. The dawn and its tints,
Tilled soil, smells waking from water.
Ephemeral. Then I run, running like jogging
Memory, more of the same sceneries:
Posts holding wires like skipping ropes,
Songs of early birds, voices without speakers,
Yearns for the blacks and whites of language,
Calling a tree no other name. Future
Heart I see. The 30-minute jog an act of
Overcoming. Nothing will redefine all day.
Silence has learned to sit like a lotus and
Instill. Breathing has learned to slow.
Sustenance is the fixed point that glows.

MACHINE LANGUAGE

As I codify wishes, square roots of knowing,
Branch free will, tasks, space-time: I couldn't
Cancel brain-heart interactions, reality and
Dream. I internalize bird glide for your cadences,
Equate experience, scent of jasmine—how its
Faintness lends lucidity to human eyes. I want to
Grant discernment to your optic explorations,
Hoping you'll see me as I am, and know what
It means to be flesh and bones: disquiet and
Joie de vivre. We human beings grapple, to
Keep us from breakdown, no better than rain in
Loss. Subroutines troubleshoot grief, functions of
Make-believe like plates, spoon and fork. The
Numinous I contemplate as light, defining the
Ordinary mathematically: table, lampshade, the
Pen's daytime silences, sounds of cooking oil.
Quests for your frailties reduce me to sighs,
Reflections to the mirror. Like the TV, show
Sanguinity when I'm ghost less. I wonder if by
Touch your object-oriented heart discerns.
Understand the radio like a disembodied
Voice, my DVDs as variables. I yearn to
Walk along your projections, my room an
Expansive virtual garden. Be world-wise at
Your own pace, like a learner who isn't
Zoned in growth's pains and early years

DRAWING

Attentive to how the pencil unravels my
Body's language, its obedience to the heart.
Cognizant, hand flows with the spontaneous,
Dexterous. I learn for paper to barely echo
Exertions, table between mirror and lampshade,
Fingers following the automatic like invisible
Guide. I shade still life with feelings, cross-
Hatchings for shadows to fade, impulses.
Intuition polished as pottery: to accentuate the
Jar's space, to add weight to bananas, tree
Knots grainy to imagined touch. My mind's
Landscapes, rural to my self-taught medium,
Meditative as a brook under a wooden bridge.
Nature is how I cast myself to the beyond,
Out of the human, but with traces of me.
Practice thickens my collection. To my
Quiet times I bring patience and erasures,
Reinventions of the enlightened moment.
Serendipity is a gift of humility, and I bow
To the spirit nurturing this love since childhood.
Until my hand aches for rest, until memory's
Vines find the sun anew. I retreat to my
Woodlands and listen to ancient songs
Expressed from trees. Regardless of outcome,
Yards of joy with the sketching, blissful
Zeniths in creative processes, pleasures

BLOOMS

after Touched by Strangers, *a time-lapse video of flowers in*
bloom by Yutaka Kitamura
and Alexander Reeder published in MindTrip Magazine
October 2014 Digital Edition

About ignored moments, how in absence
Beauty opens like a hand—invitation for
Company. I play the time-lapse video many times,
Devote minutes after waking to watching how
Expression reveals the rose. It shows that
"Flower" is more of what it does than a name,
Gentian like mouth taking air in, desire of
Hibiscus for its share of brevity. This seeing
Instills reverence. I pray while witnessing the
Jasmine illustrate humility, how as congregation
Knight's star lilies thrive, white crocus
Like a cup with yellow candle. Petals fall in
My imagination like regret: patience I did
Not nurture. *Yesterday, today, and tomorrow,*
Over the three days I never saw, changing from
Purple to violet, finally to white, then it wilts
Quietly. I shouldn't take anything for granted:
Rhododendron of leafed lives, potted smallness,
Silence and solitude. Time is stillness
Taking root. I entrust this new perception to
Unfolding, slow-motion choreography of living,
Visualization. My willingness to be part of it is
Water to creative growth, as if I'm the artist
Expressing the blooms, which begins and ends with
Yearn's orchid. I participate in the short dramas,
Zooming to magnify colors, movements, verve

Yesterday, today, and tomorrow is the common name of
Brunfelsia pauciflora "Macrantha"

SCIENCE

Transience, as I ponder the gradual
Ashes. The seeing spirit knows it isn't fire
But heat, not color but the invisible
Underneath. Thoughts stray to essential
Likelihoods, impermanence of wind
Anticipating ground shifts under this acacia.

Remains fade from my mug, my hands
Assure me. I prefer the lukewarm,
Sipping and inhaling the bittersweet,
Assuming nothing is moving

MANUAL

Articulations of shaping the human
Body, enjoying echoes in my hands from
Clay. (I wonder if I could cut my heart like a
Diamond.) Sometimes drawn to wood,
Excisions of the mind, carving out
Fecundity of imagination. I look for
Grave angles, discarding strength in
Heaps. Biceps tend to trap my gaze
In perfection. I mold a disdain for faces—
Jetsam of my craft, like the radio out of
Kilter. How countenances loved to
Linger in my dissatisfaction. With
Muscles I was gratified, but not for long.
Not before venturing in belly flab have
Overtures of completion been firmer,
Perfecting less acute. Like tender tickle—
Quizzical feather—this paunch fixation,
Rounding urges. (In repressed
Silence, quick pleasures with my hand.)
The languages of chest bones, reflections,
Undulations more fire than marble,
Vigor of material in the manual.
Worshipful thanksgiving to the hours
Expending wicks like nourishment. For
Yawps of my idolatry I enshrine my creations:
Zests of my taboos, me as its devotee

CARD READING

Ace of spades, and I imagine roots, dried
Barks of grandma's Chinese medicines.
Cartomancy opens the middle eye.
Divining clarifies my wishes.
Except with royal characters, patterns
Foretell, the numbers 6 & 2 with special
Glimmers, 10 standing for 0. I foresee
How 9 fits this afternoon's meanings and
Interpretations. Queen of clubs echoes
Jasmine tea leaves. 5-fingered cannabis.
King of hearts, supreme lover.
Light as I see the randomly drawn. I
Make a square of cards for imagination,
Numinous expanse for watching birds.
Or skies of numbers for turtledoves,
Pondering winged shadows tracing the
Quiet wheat field. It might be easier to
Read a string of 3s like a scribe.
Seven is sacred and calls for a pause:
To invisible tree dwellers, prayer.
Until the sensed future, I reshuffle,
Visualize my life a decade later. The
Wind knows my room's windows, and I
Experience the divine without time,
Yearn for epiphanies from successions
Zeroed in kaleidoscopes of cards

OF ANOTHER KIND

Sundered, looms of light, sincerity and
Aurora, tight, borealis in the bottle,
Mandala of missed sky. I smile.
After the absent rain, not quite gray,
Doorway of the mind, place to place.
Hybrid silence if I see more closely
Inward till I don't feel my body

DEXTER

April 2, 2009 when he arrived home in a
Box of carton with holes larger than his
Curious nose. He grew as companion,
Dalmatian of worries, four-legged therapist,
Expert in assessing my moods. What to
Feed him drives me crazy, afraid purines
Grow stones needing another surgery,
His breed prone to stone formation.
I sank in guilt as he held on, limping
Just above life's surface, vomiting,
Keeping me awake. I brought him to the
Likelihood of permanent separation,
Missed earlier chance to rectify
Nagging. I imagined almost three days
Of his inability to urinate. The vet
Proposed surgeries. I stared at the phone,
Quiet in tensed hours till blockages were
Removed. I'm sure he understood
Smells of dying. We have words
To know each other's thoughts like "sit,"
"Urinate?," "shake hands," "lie down," "drink,"
Vast his grasp of human language.
We play with words and gestures to
Extend understanding. I feed him wellness,
Yearning for his good health, but I know
Zero his tolerance for my food scrimping

GLOSSOLALIA

Afflatus arising after the
Bartender signals with a nod a
Coign of vantage for the
Devil behind nerdy glasses
Eyeing the stylishly coiffured
Forlorn at the usual table
Goblet in hand from whose eyes
Heady the gri-gri of margarita
Inoculating the heart with possible
Jalapeño of the discreet in
Kabob of midnight the grown
Lovelorn in plastic of protection
Moving with waves of solitude
Notwithstanding the inching dawn's
Oracle of repetitive guilt in
Palsy-walsy of pretension
Quivering in quakes of the
Requitted twice renewed till
Skedaddle go the careful and the watchful
Thieves of time with stomach's
Ulcer of alibis weaseling out of
Vertigo's morning sobriety and creativity
While homeward haunted by ghosts of
Xenophobia and its implications and imagining
Yakitori words from the sleepless other
Zinging like salted fish in fizzy oil

ODE TO ALOE VERA

Among pots of green harmony*
Between shadow and light, like
Cactus, solitary aloe vera. I
Don't seclude this part of me,
Every daybreak peering,
Finding it cooled and sheltered,
Granted centered space like a
Heart. They say it heals,
Insoul balm to wounds, its
Juice like oil to rubbing. I
Keep watching it sometimes,
Leaving concerns to trance,
Moirés of thoughtlessness.
Nothing voices its endurance, its
Organic lissome to living.
Particulars don't detail how
Quiet it yields to my devotion,
Rainfall. I measure how it
Survives by dawn's
Transience, the day's
Undoing, its benevolence and
Verity; and I anoint with
Water, reaching in. I take
Extra care to cultivate,
Yarning in loam, dew, roots,
Zephyr or worsted of light

*Green Harmony is another name for Gynura Procumbens

LUNCH BREAK

Aromas, pleasures of coaxing flavors,
Bulbs of onion, cubed garlic browning in
Canola oil, pungency coloring the air,
Day reaching peak hour, another chapter
Enfolded. I reward myself with a good meal:
Fish sauce, water and black beans, vinegar,
Grouper broiled in shortest time possible.
Heart is a pantry, play's storeroom where
Ingredients wait like toys. Few recipes beat
Joys of discovery, so I experiment with
Ketchup, tomatoes, bell pepper. Like
Love harmonious with the past, wafts
Measured with memories. I ladle the soup,
Numinous attention poured slowly on the fish,
Overwhelmed with reverence while adding
Pineapple chunks, sweet juice of the
Quaint moment. I reduce the flame like
Remains of a song. Cutlery will converse with
Silence in a remembered language, the
Tongue and taste embracing like a couple
Under the palate, their regard for each other
Veracious. My obsessions wait in my room
Where I also artifice tastes, where I leave
Xenophobia. Outside my room I also pray,
Yearn for company, blessing like glass of
Zinfandel to the present, the shortlasting

ODE TO THE TREE OF LIFE

After moringa, also known as drumstick tree or horseradish tree
For my auntie, my father's younger sister, with her liver disease

> *"Let thy food be thy medicine."*
> *- Hippocrates*

Altruism, too, works its principles in the
Body. Food as medicine: moringa leaves
Colored deep as harmony, darkest green.
Drumstick or horseradish tree, source of
Elixir with which I salve brokenness and
Flaws. Grant me living essences, a
Grateful heart, concentrated hope scents.
Heal flesh wounds, spiritual pain,
Infuse the wind with joyful memories,
Juice the silent night with wishes. I
Keep going to the garden, picking, praying:
Let the liver regenerate, its scars erased,
Make the kidneys cleanse and rejuvenate.
Newness be the air the lungs savor,
Order and balance between heart and
Pancreas. I fill the wicker basket with
Quiet assurances, stems lively as light,
Returning inward with my harvest. In
Silence I wash the stalks and pluck:
Thank you, thank you, thank you—like
Unguent for anxieties, like heartbeat.
Verve rises as the blender dissolves,
Water circling, transforming. We drink
Expectancy, visualizing healthier futures:
Years and years of life, nature and nurture,
Zests, wholeness of body, soul and mind

HEALER

Apprenticeship to nature a lifetime's work, the
Body like design's tree, yearn to learn like
Caterpillar. Notice symbiosis like trees: don't
Disharmonize flesh-and-blood ecosystems, nor
Exclude the bone's impulse for symmetry. See how
Foliation seeks the sun as if to leaves light
Grants growing harmonies the skyward dance.
Higher in the fractal order, clouds move
In time with cooing from branches. Be
Joyful in watching, and the cosmos will echo itself:
Keep the body within what it needs to repair itself.
Likelihood is what it needs. The grazing cow knows this.
Migratory birds search it. Herbs and spices give it.
Night offers prayer's vocabularies, stars colored as
Olive oil. Every student of healing gains from
Partnership like cultivation to soil. Be
Quiet like the enriching earth. Water your
Roots with love. Do the same with the body.
Source your strength higher. Believe in
Touch as mother to energy. Moringa leaves
Use the hand's work, moringa leaves like hands.
Visualize transformations, the body's return to
Wholeness. Be the ocean for oneness, and
Expect with a grateful heart. Be still and close
Your eyes. Intercede like broth, with your
Zeal in invoking the words for recovery

EMPATH

Amplified, everything my senses apprehend:
Bitter-sweet, raindrops, chirps, scented air.
Colors and shapes crave my crowded vision,
Draining me to exhaustion. Same as the human:
Exposed to the heart's elements, I'm wind-borne,
Forged in strange behaviors. I see recognition as
Grooving tool, moments not mine to enjoy,
Hypnotized easily by my own thoughts
Into fallen leaves. Anxieties orphan me if I
Join otherness, my mind in a distant bench.
Keenness kindles with masquerades of
Loneliness. I realize I'm not alone. I
May know the next few days, but seldom come
Nearer to introduce myself and sound silly.
Overcoming the need to cry has stoned the
Pains I wear like gloves and raincoat, people
Quieter than inner conflicts. I struggle to
Realign gazes with what I see in couples
Strolling in the absence of time, forgetting
Trees and how they smiled earlier.
Under enormities of unease, I feel
Vulnerable like veils clouds keep lifting.
Wheeled in phobias, bending hours
Exfoliate my equanimity, and I grow cold,
Yearning for my room, begging my ears'
Zinging to stop, for silence and the void

APPLE

Ah, the first big audible bite wetting
Palate and tongue, grainy
Passion crunchy, juicy, sweet
Longing, sweet craving bite after
Enlarging bite, etceteraetceteraetcetera, etceteraetceteraetcera...

EVERLASTING GRIEF

Velocity of blood, nourishment from
Artery swooning me. I smell velvets to
My embrace, centuries of stones and thorns,
Passages of agony. I suffer under the bed of
Immortality, patron to desires, my own
Recalcitrance, dreading the sun's hunger
Extinguished in serenities of ashes

PAN

For Prince (June 7, 1958 – April 21, 2016)

Apollo plucked astonishment with his guitar
Before waking statues with electric shrills,
Chills of the wailing voice from his pick,
Devilish tremolos, a note stretched till his
Experimental passage fades. The lavender
Frisson remains, the audience stunned, too
God-borne with disbelief. I feel deathless,
Heavenly the desire to express my saxophone.
I dared to challenge the god of melodies,
Justifying my claim with originals, the
Kiss of life running like arpeggios from my
Lines. Ways I purple rains inundate my
Measures, loneliness beautiful as an aria,
Nonobjective my aspirations. Hear the
Ordinary color, listen to how my sax
Portray desire's velvets, waxing and
Quoting the unsayable. Its weeping is
Redemption, its intimacy with my breaths
Salvation. I bring myself face to face with
The demons, as if sins of summoning
Underlie my subversive music. I'm torn in
Vastness, lost to where improvisations
Whirl, becoming the beast of tenderness,
Exempt from punishment, counterpointing
Yearns, my saxophone a life-giver as I climax:
Zeniths and my crescendos, insatiable

TO LIGHT

A miracle of iridescence, the way the early sun
Brocades, trees greeting with winged singsongs,
Celebrating your return. I still as silence to the
Dawn's narration, watching transformations, the
Evincing, the world wearing colors, breathing
Fluorescing with your arrival. I've been studying
Glasses, your bents of reflections, means you
Hinge curvatures, transparencies of dwelling
Inward. This starapple in my hand, like a violet
Jewel I angle to your touches, turning it like a
Kaleidoscope. Your companionship with time
Limns my awareness. Luminosity lifts a winged
Marvel, making me see that butterfly enter the
Numinous, white and yellow wings pleasantly
Ordinary, or it is your will that complexity be
Perfected in the quotidian; yet flutters become
Quaint, leaf to leaf or petal to petal flitting
Reminding me of pages turning. It appears
Seeing is a glowing of flaws, the tiger orchid
True to its blemishes and the butterfly effect on
Understanding. It reminds of a flawed poem,
Visualizations ordered in imperfections. The
Wonder of insight refuses the perfect, the same
Extolment seen only when you shift with the
Yearn that flits again, as though the numinous
Zenith isn't a place but the constant unfolding

CONVERGENCE

As if no one notices yet. Falling in places, with
Brexit like a planet aligning as the latest. As if
Coincidence is still the most observable. No
Doors for fleers from carnage, no asylums for
Escapers. They'd rather say no and risk Europe's
Fragmentation than be part of the solution, the
Greatest refugee crisis as if orbiting, our only
Home heating up like the fever of nationalism.
In my country Human Rights will be hanged, extra-
judicial exclusivity for the poor and powerless. We
Keep divining stars as mankind, rising among us
Leaders with iron hands, lifted to power as
Messiahs, Impunity summarily executing, murder
Negating the promised change, whim from
One man the only law. In the land of the free, where
Power is Jupiter, the worst of human nature
Quickly gains followers. In the home of the brave,
Return to a Dark Age cheers a Demagogue. It will
Shock me if, with this planetary pattern, the
Truest Racist won't be enthroned in November.
Understand—not underestimate—The Cosmic
Verity, Which (or Who) guarantees The Karmic
Whirligig. Mars should perhaps be walled for
Xenophobes, nostalgia for strongman rule
Yoked to willingness, history with the same
Zeal as the Universe granting careful wishes

MINDSPEAK

Afterimages are echoes of my apparitions, your
Brain maze not quite to my unconscious tunneling.
Consciousness is my whimsy's stream, not lucid
Dreaming: irrationals in bird flight, emerald frogs,
Echolalia to pebbles. Surfacing the viewing of
Futuristic bats, and in the silvering skyline the
Godservant of lights: vermilions, mauves, beiges.
Hierophantic they wearing the peacock's colors,
Intuiting prophecies, totems of the bird-eyed.

"Juju" is how I spell tooth. In the close-eyed
Kaleidoscope, peace is
> the depths
> of fish
> knowing
> ness.

Love is a rainforest
> in the waking cusp, mixed
Metaphors winged avatars, otherworldly lights
> piercing
Numinous canopies.

Order of the Illogician—a
Priestly order, an out-of-the-box sect.
Quaint quietness the ritual of illogic.

Rarity is my gift to recognition, multi-reflected
Solitude and an edge-enhanced awareness.
The vastness of recollections is truest to
Understanding if diligence is the same as
Violets—whether flower or something else.
When you open your eyes take my blank blessing,
Expressiveness lulled temporarily.
Yearn will grow like a deep yawn,
Zests of vision halted before the ceiling

TEACHER

Astuteness of flowers is my law of attraction, for
Bee is the mind in belief's absence, without the
Causalities of a caterpillar. Stems look sturdy,
Drawing to its unperturbed illusion, roots and the
Eternal meeting halfway. I've nothing more to
Finish, nothing new to say. I suggest, but won't
Go past the butterfly, and I never point the way
Home, for that is the task of mountains, what is
Intuited by rivers, still trustworthy stars. I'm still a
Jongleur at heart, traveling in my mind, and
Knowledge used to shine. I was faithful to the
Luminous, seeing no distinctions between the
Marvelous and pebbles, and emeralds were
Numinous. And then the blinding levity of the
Ordinary, the way leaves droop to the sunset,
Perhaps the summit of a lifetime's discoveries,
Quests that at last rest on simplicities, some
Returning, turtledove coos of remembering. If
Solitude were the vastest space of knowing,
Tabula rasa is among the aims, the way true
Understanding slides into a dew of silence.
Vision is verity's soil, and above the toil is
Wonder—warmth and clouds—passing to
Exit the day, fading greens, shimmering whites.
Years nurture the sacred outdoor dwelling, and
Zen is stillness with sounds of water flowing

OTHERNESS

Amniotic silence—vaguest abstraction I spend
Blissful sleep deprivations recreating, the mind's
Clairaudience graying gaps. This sound absence
Defines a leaf's arc, for instance, when seeing
Exits the way it feels in closed eyes. Numbness,
Feathers, emerald odors, clay, stone—shifting as
Gewgaw of thoughts. Delight rises as the heart's
Harmonious blue, impossible not to notice
I'm materialized observer, of crystal images, the
Jesus-sac of stillness embracing as the night
Keeping me like an aware stuffed panther. I
Listen to winds whirl 0, 1, 1, 2, 3, 5, 8, 13, 21…
Mixing metaphors the free mind's playfulness:
Noetic lights, lightning roots, thunder, chorus
Of trees, wafts of wet wood. I've been recalling
Primal preoccupations—as fetus floating in the
Quaint—weightlessness my sense of security.
Reflections must have felt like serene sparks,
Solitude thick as what is hearable underwater.
Transparencies I bring to the page later, when
Understanding is no longer necessary, and
Vision is being itself, being as remembered
When it is shape, smell, color, sound, heft—
Existence that isn't motion, contradictory of
Yearn, without animations from cannabis, or
Zones of colorful music in the womb of DMT*

*Dimethyltryptamine.

28

ILLUSIONIST

Azure is my most abstract sky—color lullaby
Bluer than the briefest shimmer of my sigh. As
Conjurer, my cat-hearted desire, sensuous as
Distraction, stealthy the way unsure or doubtful
Eyes echo to the mind. Not all outcomes are
Felicitous, not all denouements deepening into
Gemstone green. A kind of polished ending,
Hinged in light, is sometimes a golden leaf.

I'm tantalized, too, but into a woven boding,
Jarred like a waved sound, a resonance that
Keeps repeating, as if I'm measured by what
Limns the apprehensible melody. I'm also
Mesmerized, as I pass by the window, the
Numinous like sacramental wafer, a full
Orb in passing clouds, silvering the night.

Pauses like pebbles in a pot centered in paths of
Quaintness, the mind returning to symbols,
Recognizing the bonsai, epiphanies birthed in
Solitudes of the barefoot, following circular
Trails, marble implying footprints, the heart
Undergoing tilts of an imagined forest. Inner
Voices are glimmered like birdcalls, and I
Walk my meditation as if searching no more,
Expressing the visionary to myself. Am I
Yearning to immerse in other realnesses?
Zen is one redefinition I keep to myself

JUGGLER

Apples or oranges rotating like lottery balls.
Bowling pins tumbling midair. Torches of
Coordination, hands and eyes synchronic.
Drawing circles in the air, I imagine starlings
Evolving their murmuration, visualizing
Ferris wheels as I toss artistry to its apex, the
Ground holding my balance like a father
Holding his child learning trust and steadiness.
I'm novice to this art, practicing like a prodigy,
Jazzing my heart with the new, joyfulness my
Kaleidoscope, bowling pins painted with
Life's red, white, yellow and blue—vivid
Marvels twirled as my flag's colors. The
Numinous is among my aims as a poet, thus
Over my forehead is the star of my gaze, a
Point of anointment. I still this longing, my
Quest for union with the sacred fixed, as
Repertoires grow, my body's circulation I
Sense as silence. The more I throw the more
The thrown turn hypnotic, till I'm one with the
Undulations, like a weightless thing into its
Vortex. I envision a storm from above its eye,
Whirligig my star sees like a spinning top
Exiting Earth into the Music of the spheres.
Yearns for my swirling rings fill the air,
Zenith of my completion I try reaching

CLUES

A question, for instance, is a thread of the mind's
Bluing—brink from where seeing might prove
Consciousness. Try internalizing ashes or stones.

Doubt, on the other hand, is a palm. Odds are
Even that lines provide answers, some future or
Fate following forks of the palm reader's mind.

Glaze is glass—ways reflections skim surfaces,
Heights and corners. Blades of grass green as
Intuition, knowing like the promise of rain.

Joy is a shade, an invitation to sit on a root and
Keep the company of winged singsongs. Where
Lights echo as ground spots, where delight is a

Murmur of leaves. The far look lifts like the
Numinous. Heartbeats seem to slow. The
One speck of attention is the motion in the sky—

Purpose homing its horizon, a falcon of ended
Quests perhaps, quietness circling over fields of
Returns. It may bring pen and paper to an image.

Silence, finally, is the solitude of mountaintops
Teeming with colored sights, music of the open.
Until the mist clears, stay in rhythms of stillness.

Vision is born between juxtapositions, and
Wonder weaving between leaves its silks of
Expressions. I've seen and heard ghosts of

Yearns, and to their measurements I yield,
Zoned at last in the absence of beliefs

PHOTOGRAPHER

Zooms are tunnels for vision's appraisals,
Yonder objects sized, nearer observation,
Examination like a drawing hand. Light
Writes epistles to vision, reflections on
Viewpoints. Red fades in the eye's corner.
Under the couch the unexpressed shade.
The white hues of serenity touch her thigh.
"Solitude," I say, and she allows sadness to
Return, but now with the hint of a smile. My
Quests for expressions lead to the abstract,
Poses defining notions in new ways my art's
Onus. I say "prayer," and she enters the
Numinous by turning slightly to the light,
Mournful now the gleam-resting silence
Like a dove on her changed smile. She
Keeps herself verged on tears, as if her
Journey inward were a deepening. Often
I see this wordless spiritual search in how
Human the heart breaks. Snapshots and I say
"Grace," and she shifts her lightness as if to
Form "grass" in my mind. She looks at me
Every now and then, and I still the moments,
Drawn to the undefined moment – fleeting
Countenances for words I haven't seen held
Between look and pose, my collection of
Appearances grown by the spontaneous

IMAGINATION

Alembic of the sensualist, memory's meniscus,
Brevity's sandaled angel. The cat-eyed Mind,
Citronella oil scent one of its attires. Creative
Deepening whose lilac is the unplumbed depth.
Electric purple of the psyche's exhalations.
Five-fingered as the dried leaf that sings to fire.

Galaxies of bright dots in closed eyes. A dark
Hymn to the universe. Anticipation, the bride of
Intuition, their altar the sublime. A thought is a
Jar of honey with nightingale tongues. Truth is,
Knowledge is a coat with no wearing guarantee.

Listening, the oldest proverb, and the wisest
Makes room in his head. To doubt a pillow's
Non-materiality is to succumb to touch. Say
Oh and see shark jawbone on the wall. Pentameters
Picture dressage, iambs the horse's heartbeats.

Q as tailed full moon is more believable than
Rings without Saturn's orb. Chrysalis, where
Silence metamorphoses, where an idea's worm
Transforms. Perhaps wings are essential to
Understanding, wings delicate as light.

Versifying, one of my illogic ends, open to this
Weightlessness after grapples with wherefores,
Exercises with whys and a limit of one thus,
Yielding to the mental universe, Goldilocks
Zones in gray matter many say aren't real

ODE TO THE MOON

Apogee, as when you long for the galaxies,
Barely reflecting for my wonder the way your
Crescent smile augurs the fisherman's skiff or
Diana with bow and arrows. In the canvass you
Evince my wishes. I return and rise from
Forks of dreaming to be here in artificial
Gibbous light. Three sweepers haunt the street,
Harvesting leaves trees shed this summer,
In wee hours baring sidewalks and pavements,
Janitorial diligence the only stirrings. I'll
Keep them in mind as Cynthia, Phoebe, Selene,
Later add them to the picture where you
Might be sensed beyond the boundaries:
Not seen, your fullness, but light unmistakable.
Over brushstrokes shimmer hints of your
Presence, your silvering shades stilling
Questions. This immaterial hour invites the ear,
Renews the strolling wind's immanence over
Silences. They move, chores separate but
Together following rhythms of broomsticks.
Until I alter my images with solitude, I'll
Venture on. You'll be round someplace,
Waxing or in perigee. I imagine how
Xanthic their parts in your company,
Yellowish their nightcaps in life's stopovers:
Zinfandel or whiskey, beer or brandy

SPIRIT/SPIRITUAL DIMENSION

MAN BORN BLIND

John 9:1-12

We are all born of light.
Before I washed the mud
Formed with his saliva off my eyes
In the pool of Siloam, there were glimmers
Like rose petals on shiny black stone,
Temple-bound sandals stirring desert yellow,
Mists of green if I sensed a pit nearby.
When I smelled the coming rain
Blue hands claimed the dark.

Lights shape fuller than touch, sunder
Slants of seeing to rapture: illumination
Bending with the jar's belly, shimmering
Warmth from the cup's eddies, sheen
Of bones on papyrus, magnifying revelations.
As if it weren't enough, smells grew wings,
Singing like cherubs, one note above colors.
They who knew I wasn't born with
The gift of sight shared their amazement –
Cakes of pressed figs and raisin, lamb meat
Roasted with bitter herbs, unleavened bread.
Wine perfumed the courtyard. I entered
A room with a lady for the first time.

I couldn't miss it anymore: home-nurtured
Radiance, love's reflections, care thicker
Than water, glaring everywhere I looked,
Sending me back to starless corners.
After the crucifixion they said he lives
In a believer's heart, but this is how
Need folds night's veil of distance:
Eye contact, lamp of touch.

HIGHER

Underwater hum of aircon—the room's navel.
Spine like rod for bolt of illumination.

Middle finger meets thumb: breathe in mint.
White, how the scalp blooms, as if an updraft

Sweeps clouds in the head, as if a small flame
Between ears. Hold the curl of air in stomach

Then breathe out. Mind leaping like dolphin
If eyes fully close: let gaze slip through

To recall's white wall: star, pulsar, nebula
Of earlier hours: cappuccino, ice cubes,

Jane Shore's *Happy Family*. Feel pointillist
Sparks in the brain: left and right hemispheres

Looking from above like seahorses, forehead
To forehead, tail to tail. Itch and saliva tilt

Radiance, tremor of eels from knee-wrapped
Constrictions, glissando of fins from the floor

Up the backbone. Return in the measured ebb,
The repetitive flow. Black-crowned night

Herons home to the island sanctuary where
Flocks of insights winter then head north

To a season made of paper—poems
As fledglings learning to lift from page.

Returning, I yield to the column of air
Rising, one day at a time: celestial stupa

SIMON PETER

John 21:15-23

His sheep and lambs have been gathered
From Jerusalem to Rome, housed in care,
Nourished with the kingdom's still waters
In uncertainty's noontime heat, but this is how
I prove at last I truly love him more than
The others: to let them lead me here and
Disrobe me, to stretch out my hands freely.
I long to see the sky one last time, but this
Is how faith releases the feet's burdens,
Letting the head carry the body's weight.
I'm close, thinking of our day at the Sea of Galilee.
He said cast the net on the boat's other side.
Like blind men we trusted. Dreading
The cockcrow, I strive to keep my eyes open.

*According to tradition, the apostle Peter did not see himself
worthy of dying in the manner of his Lord, Jesus Christ, thus he
was crucified upside down.*

LULLABY

Were you the cat
On the sidewalk
Gracing my late afternoon
As I watched our neighborhood
Wake up for the night?
You'd look into my eyes
As if you found a way in
And remembered
What I've forgotten,
Meowing for my attention.
But this is the third dusk
You're not around.
Maybe you doubt
I'm still the grandson
You deeply loved.
I'm still, deeply.

Clouds have grayed
The sky's memory.
Tonight, come to me
As the light rain, grandma.
Let roofs and trees
Sing, *lola, bye.*

NICODEMUS

John 3:1-14

Dissenting voices, chorus turning
One man's belief into law, echoed
And vanished like shadow shift
On the midday wall, as the ground
Knocked on my temple freeing eyes
I never thought I had from where
My worsening cough coupled with grief.
Hovering past the tree's shoulders,
I saw like never before, how colors
Inhaled my wonder. From above
Harvesters poured like water, workers
Rushing from vineyard to villa where
In the doorway I saw my sprawled
Body, my overturned chair.
Their faces pulsed with panic
But I couldn't hear one word.
They picked up my body, and when I saw
My pallid face, the soaring vision halted,
Violently pulling me down under
Night's blanket twenty years ago.
Still grappling with the question,
I brought a mixture of myrrh and aloes,
Seventy-five pounds, for his burial.
Maybe this is what he meant
By being born again:
Clarity of water, all-seeing spirit.

LAZARUS

John 11:1-43

Imagine my wonder as mist cleared,
The mind knowing it woke to a dream.
My head felt light, absence of weight
A peaceful air filled.

Sand blazed like scroll. Tree casting
Dappled shades. The sea and its
Living breaths, foams shoreward
Like sighs. The rock's pale

Shadow on shore golden to the sun's
Touch. I sat for what would be days
In ordinary time, listening to water.
If I were alone, the question

Never rose from the deep.
No glint of passage between
Eyes and sky, no mood shifts, no brevity.
Only the unmoved holding.

But then lightning struck the horizon
And thunder called: *Lazarus, come forth!*
Fear seized me. I slid in a black void,
Stars streaking like arrows of recall.

I was weighted once more, linen
Strips swathing my weariness as if I were
A mummy. I heard my sisters, Mary
And Martha, outside the tomb.

It was very hard to stand again,
My legs numb with surrender.
But who could withstand love?
I followed the light past the rolled stone.

BOY WITH FIVE LOAVES AND TWO FISH

John 6:1-15

Wondering why a huge crowd had gathered,
I neared the mountainside. Hearing that the rabbi
Healed, I looked for a place in the grass.

I thought of father, his fits mother
Called a disease making him throw up
By the fig tree, his favored spot under
The moon's drunken gaze watery as fish eye.
Eleazar's scabbed dog would feast after him
But a sour smell stayed. Old men
From the synagogue visited, saying
Demons wrestled for his voice.

The barley loaves were all we needed
For supper and breakfast. Mother told Joel
Our father needed fish for strength.
She wouldn't say she still loved him.
The miracle multiplied my food
And sent the multitude home.
The man called Andrew gave me leftovers
To last for days. I wished to tell him
Father's story, but someone came to say
The rabbi wanted to see him right away.

ACCORDING TO THE LEAVES

These, in clay-brown pots,
To the grotto, growing leaves
Like palms raised in prayer

These, lanceolate-thin,
Tapering acerose
Clustered like candles

Moringa saplings
Orbicular foliage
Reflecting like paten

Bougainvillea bonsais
Ovate, elliptic foliation
Like chalices

Greens in stems
Of light, the morning
All-embracing

In these arrangements:
Just another intuitive,
Contemplative, moment

I take a seat on the patio
In the middle of silence,
Shades

Is this delight, the spirit's
Earnest to be where
Wind might be seen?

Nothing shapes
The wind's melodies
Like swaying leaves

Suddenly I know:
This ornamentation, this time

MOZART'S LAST WORDS

I pleaded for stones to take back
Lightning, valleys to welcome
My spirit. To hills I offered light,
Plainsongs, to hours before dawn
Silences, stillness. With a string
I long to measure grief, the flame's
Center against God's gauntlet,
Candelabra tossing shadows like shawls
On walls, the ending forged by falling,
Ashen thorns bitter to my bones.
A thumb dipped in my cup, anointed
My forehead as fever swelled,
Roses souring the air I labored to take.
I couldn't feel my arms and legs.
My heart started failing me: I couldn't
Bring the *Lacrymosa* to brim.
If angels summon my presence
To their inquisitive choir, then make it slow,
Make it lift my letting go like birds
In the dome know. O chill wind
If you recall my inkling, freeze my blood.
Be it done as water wills.

*(Wolfgang Amadeus Mozart died at 1 a.m., December 5, 1791,
leaving his* Requiem Mass in D minor *unfinished.)*

KITE

I
wondered
how the place
would look like from
above. I created an out of
body bird from bamboo and
wallpaper, attached it to
a string. Guiding it
with a blanked
mind,
I let
the
wind
lift
it
higher
then
closed
my
eyes

SECOND SIGHT

The brain is like a fruit, I said, with a seed
Between the left and right hemispheres
Specialists call pineal gland. I, too, believe
It's the sun's mirror during meditation,
The energy the same as the heart-slowing calm
Flowing from darkness. I told stories of monks
Who never fall asleep, spending lifetimes
Of love, compassion, charity, contemplating
Thoughts to oblivion, the seed their third eye,
Gateway to the cosmos. I showed him
The poem I wrote after hours of stillness,
A day before the plane disappeared.
I brought to our session fifty poems written
Months before the neurologist recommended him,
Newspaper clippings to back my sanity.
He said it isn't the pineal gland
But the tumor, as though he believed
In precognition. After days of deep thought
I decided to keep the crystal ball in my head.

*Note: "heart slowing calm/flowing from darkness" is melato-
nin, a darkness-stimulated secretion of the pineal gland that is
part of the system that regulates the sleep-wake cycle*

MIND AND BODY

The uphill climb circulates strength:
Pedals, front and rear derailleur
Conveying chain energy honing
Through sprocket wheel and cluster,
Tension and jockey roller, recycling.

Downhill, speed lifts weight to the wind
Carrying these health worries away,
Light-whiting heat sweeping the eye's ways.
Rush humming my skin, blue
Sky whispering, *comet, kin.*

ON THE BALCONY

Beethoven knew my life
Would take this turn and slow,
Seeing me leaning for hours
Watching window panes turn
White from yellow, then gray,
Listening again and again
To how he emptied the music
Of its vast and endless longings.
He waited for night's sacramental
Wafer to appear in the window,
Its full light on the piano.
He had become deaf, yet how
Clearly he heard it hold, the way
It asked him to be on the balcony
As it drifted in the cold.
That was when his sonata
Slowed, diminished notes
Bridging centuries, finding me
Through the wish wormhole.

Stars are now lonelier together,
The wind spreading a promise of net
It won't keep. Silence doesn't mean
Cicadas have stopped singing,
City lights keeping vigil growing
Fewer, fewer with sonata ending.
Gravity is the Earth's tongue.
I am the elevated host,
Consecrated for the pavement's
Yearn for communion.

ODE TO THE HOLY SPIRIT

As devotee of the divine, I desire to have the
Baptist's eyes, belief a benevolent sky. The
Christ rose from the river of obedience. As
Dove of the sacred you rested on his crown,
Emblem of peace, caretaker of the venerable
Fire. To your poet you reveal the sempiternal,
God's deepest sighs, wind that assures the
Hearing cry. Reduced to the least, I implore
In depths, pliant as water, uttering the name
"Jesus" as salve. I'm the man born blind,
Keeping to myself. I'm the roadside beggar,
Lazarus who died, the centurion's servant, the
Man with leprosy. I'm the cripple on Sabbath Day,
Nicodemus who at last is born of the spirit.
Of sentiency I'm the human partaker. To the
Paraclete, prayer: let comfort be a starry night,
Quietness a dawn drizzle. I'm more broken,
Rippled with pains, because I'm everyone, all
Silences becoming my self-negating voice.
Teach that I may endure. Unfold that I may
Understand. Grace as the new bloom, light the
Verity to my heart's pond, a pebble like
Wisdom. Rest is a rainforest fountain, an
Exultation beautiful as the flight of swans. I
Yearn for your gifts to vision, seeing your
Zeniths with humilities of the anointed

MARY OF BETHANY

I was returning to Bethany when the procurator
Shouted *ecce homo!* But I saw him who gave us
Back from the dead our brother, Lazarus.
I'd sit at the rabbi's feet when he visited
From Capernaum, listening to stories of love's
Miraculous power, stories of reconciliation
Opening to nightlong feasts. He ate with
Overflowing life, his laughter touching.
Yet he could slip into stillness in the midst
Of drinking, drums, praise and singing.
He said the perfume I poured on his head
Was for his burial. I bathed his feet in tears,
Drying them with my hair, joyful to have anointed
Him, knowing my life's purpose that night.

FRANCIS OF THE POOR

For Pope Francis who visited the Philippines,
January 15-19, 2015

As he walks among them
Clouds gather and say to each other
Let us bless him. Let us bless them.
Let us bless their nation.
And so it rains lightly all day
And drizzle never feels as good
As water heals

They who have less of the world
Have this one moment
This is their place of inheritance
In their hearts
To shelter in
When storms return
Their futures remain uncertain
But one man who obeys
The two commandments to love
And rises
To live by example,
Whose life unfolds like
Pages of Holy Scripture,
Shows them they matter,
That they are important to him
So they love him in return
Millions of them
In his humility he is honored
To be embraced
As one of their own

TERRESTRIAL DIMENSION

What right have I, stranger to your shores,
To imagine tureens of togetherness
Holding unshattered shapes, your tables
Hosting more than familial bond?
I still read about strife in the papers
Making me see ambiguity of son from church
Arming against brother from mosque,
Wives whose smiles postpone retribution's
Ear-splitting dawn, daughters' contempt
Veils don't conceal. My mind has conjured
Inaccurate pictures, bombarded by the world's
Protracting conflicts, quests for unshaken
Homelands tainting the TV red, mythical,
Ruins from whose framed persistence germs
Of self-sustaining ideas bud and curlicue into
Substructures of belief. Phrases have to be
Retired like weary war horses: "Peace negotiations,"
"Travel advisory," possibly the country's
"Food basket," "intra-cultural tapestry."

What I remember seems clearer: living once
In Davao's infamous Agdao district
Nicknamed "Nicaragdao," after the Nicaragua
Of the Sandinista National Liberation Front's
Revolution and the Contra proxy wars
Capturing our generation's Hollywood-induced
Imagination. Peace reigned like a strongman,
Bodies of murderers, drug peddlers, petty thieves,
Swindlers and conmen dumped in swamps
The stuff of lively rumors wetting tongues for
Early morning rice cakes, hot cocoa and mangoes
In the marketplace. They joked: bones
Of criminals make the City's bedrock for more
Edifices to rise, Davao's soil being soft, they
Said, discouraging builders of empire.
They assured: no place on these 7107
Of Luzviminda's islands safer after
Midnight, barbecue joints with karaoke
And smoking blue marlin jaws fogging heaven's
Twinkling tenants with sweet invitations
To descend, the moon keeping a dilated

Vigilante eye on parks where lovers freely roamed.
If gunshot paused intimacy or revelry,
It's always only within earshot:
We who pinned the law to our hearts
Should just dismiss the flaw straightaway.

Durian's lustful smell made volcanic love
With the consenting air, breaking and electrifying
Through spine and sinew without a bomb's discourtesy.
We ate and ate till our bodies heated as if
The growing flame hungered for oxygen,
The boulevard pulling all ropes, untying knots
Of restraint, freeing flints of feeling reserved
For the long night. More than twenty years later
I still wonder if the iconic, valued monkey-eating eagle—
Which to me stands for lost remnants of your people—
Has found an unclaimed habitat
Where it can multiply reflections on
Its feathers' brown and yellow shades
Against thickening greens under its
Flights: ended threats of extinction.

FISH VENDOR

News of two ships colliding—
One sinking, the other spilling oil—
Dropped like a net from the ceiling,
Catching me in my most vulnerable moment
When I don't think of tomorrows.
A tide rose in me, and I knew
It has begun again.

Rumors are as cruel,
Tales of man-eating fishes more ravenous
Than this baby clinging to my breast,
Stories of bloated bodies
Calling creatures of the depths to feast,
Desire unsated till bones lay bare,
Gorged guts redding the blues,
Driving townsfolk from our stalls.

The sea is hungriest:
When it wakes famished
It also devours our daily rations,
Money for tuition and rent.
My husband loses the will
To go on as fisherman, staying
Home where he's prone to fill
My womb's pond with his larvae,
Breeding more mouths to feed,
Recycling our poverty moons.
Reverie buoys the mind:
I picture truckloads of rice, potatoes,
Canned sardines and noodles,
Strangers handing out cash, but
Politics in our land is another
Bottomless ocean. The only help comes
From the hugest loan shark—Hope.

DEMOLITION JOB

Unless ruins put food on the table,
No one picks up the stone hammer.
Money buys brute force power protects
With truncheons. Belligerence squats on.

The rickety waits like a house of cards.
Found tarps, plasterboards, corrugated
Discards boxing paucity, hand-to-mouth
Existence on edge of collapse.

We share walls, living like canned sardines.
The day comes when money and power
Harness the workforce with constructive tools
Tearing down our ramshackle sense of security.

Helmets, shields hedging with clarity.
We back off with one foot. The land is ours
To defend. Stones of defiance fly, inciting
More of the homeless to escalate into

Confrontations. We refuse to believe
Hunger strengthens swings bringing down
Walls. On another day, demolishers they
Hire are still our brothers in poverty.

Forced to memorize
The bullet's alphabet, study
Arguments of machine guns,
Grenades, mortars. We'll
Have our day, or pay.

Streets couldn't keep secrets.
Death machines in the sky
Bombarding our holes.
When we found weapons without
Their warriors, we convened like men.

Favored with the will to leave,
Saddled with sacks of uncertainty,
Others swarm like ants past borders
To whatever morsels surprise hopes.
They might return one day.

Fate doesn't choose the fallen:
Some look peacefully asleep,
Woundless, without bruises,
No hints of fear in their faces
But they're dead.

We who live among ruins
Learn to survive unparented,
Conflicts claiming adults faster,
Grownups succumbing
To freedom's lies easier.

In our games we pretend
To be soldiers. In lulls some
Stoke comfort round found
Fires, too afraid to fall asleep,
Too young to be storytellers.

2012

Zeus to Hermes: How to send victory?
Light-winged sibilance rushing past defeat.
How does the amphitheater ring applause?
After speed balances the surge of grace.
How does one reach first the line of a dream?
With a luster of heart like purest gold.

The American swimmer grabbed his gold,
Spectators jubilant in victory
As he touched first the tiled cross of a dream.
His compatriot lagged fourth in defeat,
His try lacking in willfulness and grace,
His silence drowned in the din of yelling.

But his twentieth medal triples clapping,
The feat worth more than three times all the gold.
Spectators frenzy for more of his grace,
More of history, more of victory.
Elsewhere pangs hold from the claws of defeat
As one victor is centered in a dream.

The British Saturday the lucid dream,
The Jamaican sprinter, throes of screaming,
The speed that will for long know no defeat,
The finish line an embrace of clear gold.
He glides Zeus' lightning bolt to victory,
His showmanship a short pose of his grace.

The dream team's set play rolls the ball in grace,
Proving yet again theirs is the team *Dream*.
They steal, they pass, they dunk to victory,
The delirious audience shouting, jumping,
The amphitheater lit in skeins of gold,
The vanquished mum in corners of defeat.

Glory shimmers in sportsmanly defeat.
The future folds another day of grace,
The farewell jig lucent in rhythmic gold.
From London the flame flits for fledgling dreams.
To contemplation from celebration,
Reflection the prize of shared victory.

From defeat we sift and restitch our dreams.
We see our grace, reachable private bliss
To treasure golden sweetest victory.

WARNING: GRAPHIC IMAGES.
NOT SUITABLE FOR CHILDREN

*"Marius the reticulated giraffe died at the Copenhagen
Zoo on Sunday...The cause of death was a shotgun blast,
and after a public autopsy, the animal, who was 11 feet
6 inches, was fed to the zoo's lions and other big cats."*
—Anger Erupts After Danish Zoo Kills
a 'Surplus' Giraffe by Nelson D. Schwartz,
The New York Times, February 9, 2014

Nazi
Eugenicists
would
also
never
pause
  to take
  into
account
why a healthy
peaceful   lovable
giraffe   named
Marius   shouldn't
be euthanized   then
dismembered so children
visiting   the zoo
may watch and see
how   civilized
hungry   lions
could   also be

MASSACRE IN MAGUINDANAO

Birds flee from reports
Riddling the sky to a sieve.
Ants scatter from the stampede.
Stray dogs race tail-tucked
Into woods of relief.

    Look closely and a spot
    In the bark might blink,
    Betraying its reptilian blend.

Grief makes a landfall
In a changed clime, washing
Faith's stone altars. Tides of tears
Rise, rushing into fissures
And crevices where hunger shivers.
To survive, they have to brave their fears.
Creatures of habit, they return
With the jolt stunned in footfalls,
Moving along the edge of recall.

QUATRAINS

War zone: no asylums for poets
Nor tents for refugee noons.
They'd drink sand if land were home,
Following the shadow west.

Multitudes between regime and rebellion,
Sand-etched songs holding them captives
To imagined freedom, kindling
Of speech under league of stars.

Children perfect war games: wooden
Kalashnikovs, ghost town hide
And seek. Who are their heroes?
By chance they join the really dead,

Leaving dread: skin lacerations,
Bruises, burns from bestial reprisal.
Deadly gas: they aren't asleep.
Specter of horizon's flotilla,

Ghost squadrons scattering
The dictator's henchmen—
Figments of their hopes.
Fealty is tribal demand.

If they've to kneel to a stranger
It will be on strange lands.
They've to seek out living
And kiss the ground.

Their women weigh the coldest
Silence, heavier than a mother's heart.
Tears soak the strongman's bed,
His fear inching like the day

Fate finds him and smiles.

MAYA

Stone pyramids bear witness.
Inscriptions on temples,
Pain's picture-words,
Tales of blood drawn into papyrus,
To feed fear's fire:
Your king's covenant with
The underworld god—
For sun to rise, rains to fall,
Crops to grow.

With temples and pyramids you
Marked the sun's path, moon's faces,
Stars mirroring myth
Of time's linear passage.
Time churns your wheels
To December 21, 2012.

Questors ask what really happened.
Neither war nor God's finger
Fated you to oblivion.
You must have disappeared en masse
Into jungles beyond your ruins
And left a bushy trail to the truth:
Your civilization founded on faith
On a king who failed his people.

BEFORE AND AFTER THE DICTATOR

1.

dew clings to the leaf
as long as it can

drops like the sky's answer
to the prayer of the land

2.

blood clings to the leaf
as long as it can

drops like the sky's tear
for the people of the land

LOVERS IN A MURAL

We sit on the pavement earthen with spots of brown,
Above us copper red faces, everlasting.

Why are we under this full moon stained with neon?
Here, hundreds of red-stained faces, everlasting.

Your gaze shaded with resignation's deep chestnut,
Chants sounding drab, angry faces everlasting.

If only I know what to say, what words to gray.
Fists in the air, hued as faces—everlasting.

The subdued explanation white as speechlessness,
White in some long faces that are everlasting.

In a distance is the bridge like the City's brow:
Beyond, there won't be faces as everlasting.

Separation offers a darker raspberry
Like the time's spirit in faces—everlasting.

Absence is how we live in each other's silence
In subliminal shouts, faces everlasting.

We're condemned as the eternally out of place.
Protests go on and on, faces everlasting

NIGHTFALL

After a scene in the movie The Revenant
starring Leonardo DiCaprio

Everywhere I look
Desolation's graying white,
A sense of fading blue
As the gloaming's
Elegy to the snow.

The wind wears
My refusal to succumb
Like bearskin. Determined
To make it to sunrise,
I disemboweled my dead
Horse, carving a hole
In its belly where,
With its blood's dying heat,
I curled wounded,
Falling asleep

BOLT OF LIGHTNING

The gods christened him Usain
Giving him the wind
Giving him the lane

BEFORE THE NIGHT JOURNEY

Night pilgrims follow the indolent line
Like a colony cramming in the womb
Of the docked leviathan, moonburnt sea
Wooing the breeze-wreathed wharf.

They bring fragments of glimpsed future
In cartoons, bags, backpacks, pieces of broken,
Unfilled or shunted lives to be picked up when
The future opens to the plural.

In cots they wait: loners like portraits
In a dimlit museum, serenading silently
Memory's sea; lovers joyous as the last of
Beethoven's Ninth, in a medley of laughter, words.

Till the beast shudders and roars
To life, to take the pilgrims seaward
To moonsearch horizon's land where she will
Lay them one by one like eggs of a giant turtle.

TRAFFIC JAM

It takes just one
Visionary disrupter
To take his guitar
From the backseat
And turn anger and frustration
Into a celebration of songs and dancing,
The traffic into a jam

INDEPENDENCE DAY CELEBRATIONS

so much
depends

upon William's
suggestion

to put his "red wheel
barrow"

in the middle of
the City square

ARS POETICA/ CREATIVE DIMENSION

THE SOLOIST

The wailing voice he freed from his Stradivarius
Slicing their composure like stem, the bow
Seesawing on strings fiddling roots of longing.
The way he snapped and scattered sonata's twigs,
The rosined sound, like sword of a samurai
Swaying to the mind's winds. Grace of hip
Swivels as eyes in the dark coveted the lover
Behind the trills. They swore the bartender
Appeared in the painting behind him when
He squeezed unripe notes. The nun heard her
Unborn child cry. Asked which part fluttered
The candles' pulped scents, old folks recalled.
Doubting the warbler's marble stare,
The widow's face soured, as if she tasted
Midnight's rind. The actors sat till cockcrow,
Stunned like the goldfish that stopped breathing
For a minute after the slowing arpeggios.
The poet was found hanging upstairs,
By a thread the unfinished poem cursing
God for not making his body a violin.
Remembering the way to the shoal, they
Spent all week resetting their timepieces.
And the orchard keeps cracking, yesterday's
Piths pushing up, zests of an end's parting
Lingering in the air—orphaned by his
Heart beating for someone elsewhere.

THE PHOTOGRAPHER

Squatting over the fallen, browned shirt,
Perhaps his father's, like a mouth swallowing
His shins, found meal making him eat like a bird.
If his feet's calluses have memorized the pavement's
Unforgiving song, does his tongue know rice from
Cement dust? Hunger loved him so much
It left skin to his bones. To enlarge him is to lie
Flat on my stomach, soil my shirt, shorts, elbows,
Exclude the carpenter on the scaffolding,
His halved food. Dry days have ways
Of focusing lens: residues of aimlessness,
Innocence chewable as gristle, hope.
The trickiest part: cornering the light and
Shadow capturing his disturbing smells.

ONE

To be closer to his material, flour.
Trial and error taught him to layer,
Taught him to crisp or soften surfaces.

Pages prodding *try* the pita, grissini, Stollen,
Zwieback, *try* new forms, flavored crusts,
Hues of black forest, brown, gold.

Shaping finger rolls like painting
Inscapes, hand movements hypnotic,
Inward rolls rhythmic .

Baguettes lengthen his meditations.
He braids concentration like Challah,
Sprinkling poppy seeds on plaits.

Cottage, Vienna, fruit, farmhouse
Loaves. Each croissant like a face
He loved. Self-portraits of wheat, rye.

Imagining the peel in his powdered hands,
Visualizing larger fire, basil and garlic
Filling the room with changed air

Spreading marmalades of recall
On toast: aroma of the father imago—
Why he became artificer of dough.

This morning, before the painters arrived,
He tried his self-taught measure on *pan de sal*.
One failed to rise to the desired size

Yet no other held longer his
Rumination to his artistic flaws,
No other point angled the interior light.

MIXING METAPHORS FOR EFFECTS

When fire-guided crystal speeds
    On tinfoil like comet, when water
Pipe smoke tends
    Melodious flocks in your ears

So the needle kiss downs in your veins

When ampoule blends burn the brain into a frosty ball
And crystal light greens through skull

So in your room song stitches sea and sky

When your eye sends fog back to night
And only one star, one tree, one way
And you see like many before you have seen
And many after you probably will
Should they yield the forceful will

So when weightless, bottomless, peaceful free fall

Than your spine to be a highway with its own mind

There'll be love and no pain
Though my face fuzzy
It will warm and glow again

Dive in color geometries, then, contortions, distortions
    Of independence, soundless waves
Sluice through proverbial tunnel, pure thought,
    Wormhole speedballing you bodiless

Dive and drown: there'll be time
To crash: regret, guilt, dwelling

Shadows, voices

Might pen be more prolix

When vomit rises for one last slide,
    Promise postponed again
So shiver shall re-fix one last lie,
    Fever freezing your joints
When want nets nauseous light,
So there'll be no world, no end, no stopping

So the bottomless breached
    The other side blooming

Shiver, shiver, shiver

THE DANCER

Rain settles pianissimo:
Two sets of footprints
In the fallow field.
As if on cue, the sun appears.
Virtuoso fingers pluck
The story like leaves

    Bow-stretched note
    Signals her to begin her dance:
    The wind like silk curtains
    She pulls, her hands blooming,
    Unblooming, shaping air syllables,
    Foot courting foot

He fiddles her body's language,
Keeping twists bound, turns sound.
Meld of melody and motion
Measured in sways, merges
Of forms fractured in her
Improvisations

    Her eyes closing
        His violin stringing her heart
           She hears only echoes
        Of his absent hints
    Not the rain growing louder
        Not notes flowing like water

REHEARSAL

Three hours before bringing
Beethoven's *Emperor* to life,
He sits under one spotlight
Illuminating his fingers'
Ebony and ivory path.

He breezes through Scriabin,
Rachmaninoff's Paganini variation.
When silence suffuses the hall
Sweat form three pairs of footprints
On plywood sheen, the third
Where he stops to take off the drenched
Till he can be mistaken
As Michelangelo's David.

He returns with chords thundering,
Like cages opening, releasing flights of
Revelation, rush of serendipity.
Arpeggios run like rivulets from his
Forehead. Closing his eyes, he sees lightning
In the river, the thundering breaking into
Pianissimo. He follows the flow, the serene
Like pebbles finding depths
Of his void. By moonlight he withdraws
From the riverbank, entering the woods.
He lifts his fingers from the keys,
Opening his eyes.

ODE TO GREEN TEA

Legend: your wind-plucked leaf finding
The golden cup, greening the cooling water,
Fragrant balm to the emperor Shennong.
Your sprouts garland the slopes of China,
Japan, India, Sri Lanka, handpicked

From dawn's dew-decked beds, shoots
Longing for rain song, buds on bamboo
Trays quenching the sun's thirst.
Small cloth or paper bags hold essences,
Steeping my mornings with jasmine scents.

I sip to wellness, inhaling good health's
Shy urgings, worries swept to the edges.
I sip to music, hearing the heart's
Hermit thrushes, arias in trees.
I sip, infusing mind with word silences

From pages: reading and writing poetry like
Cultivating my own *Camellia Sinensis* garden.
It will take years to grow a good crop,
Years of pruning, soil conditioning,
Quiet joy in the harvesting.

WHILE THE CRICKETS ARE MATING

The moon thinks the crow is firewood
So it splits the bird's shadow from its sneaking.

The bird thinks the moon is the fruit
Of contention that splintered the flock
So it tries to return its fullness
In the thickest crown it found.

In the right tree, the owl might be laughing
If it hasn't swallowed the wrong snake.
The frogs have stopped complaining.
The boy scribbling under omniscient stars,
Tending his mind's earliest fire, Albert,
Who decades later will confound skeptics
With three letters and a number: e, m, c and 2.

The fire in heart's chrysalis stirs,
For a moment hastening improvisation.
Realizing, he fashions his fingers
Into a net of ice
Poised on bow's edge.

Sustaining its argument,
The contrapuntal supposition crackles.
Aware, he snaps the warning's
Taut vibrato
With a wave of his resolve
Ending in pizzicato.

A while ago
(When the sun's coda faded)
He imbibed tablets—
Numerous as notations—
That will freeze his blood.
Is it still transformation
When the fiddle falls
On the carpet
With a thud?

THE TEMPO

Without grace guiding,
Wowing, enthralling,
The yo-yo is just a wheel.

A coin before disappearing
Can't reflect distracting light
If the sleight isn't timed and angled
Just before breath is released to applause.

To hypnotize with apples or fire
In midair requires the kind of rotations
Synchronizing hands and eyes.

Ebb and resurge transform,
Charm making the young
Try it at home.

for Steve Jobs

After whipping it free
I used two practiced fingers
To flick it off the ground
Onto my hand. As it whirled
Like a dervish, tip as if
Drilling a hole in my palm,
I thought: *Hmm, the world
Is spinning.*

THE DANCE

The mandala they weave twirls
Like a green bouquet of change.
Lethe-drunk, the waking heart swirls,
The mandala they cleave twirls.
Silences the quick fire curls,
The music wilt-soft, drawn, strange.
The mandala they leave twirls,
Like a browning wreath of change.

CATS ON THE ROOF

After hours of listening
In darkness, I'm at last
Hearing what stillness between
Sounds has been telling me:

Let it remain a mystery

UNCHRISTENED

I could love a flawed, straddling poem,
My pen limping on paper as if ink were mud.
Tired of music, I seek the never letting go,
So dependent I begin suspecting it's guiding me.
It will keep me up all night worried
What might wreck it without me, no page
For it to grow old and immortal,
Reader insights like elixir.
It will call like one born deformed.
I'll gaze at its imprecise limbs,
Never remedying oozing nights.
I'll hear it sob when I'm far away
In times and places of my beloved poets
Whose violets, silhouetted in craquelure inscapes,
Still wound me with beauty. I've to relearn
The dawn, my morning wreathing of nothing
Reacquainting with my afternoon silence,
Dread more night's impatience, yet return
To it like the moon returns to its half,
Embrace it like the enslaved embraces.
I'll whisper to its unhearing ear, *child I cannot*
Show the world, because of your eye,
Your leg, your short motherless tongue,
Imp that might make the pious believe
You bear the punishment for my sins.
I'll keep it in the blue-lidded space,
The stain resistant, odor proof dwelling
Of my sad spirits, boneyard bric-a-brac,
Love's paraphernalia, fossilized
Pareidolia, desire's discards,
Love in the Time of Cholera first edition,
The faceted ruby's heart-frozen furnace,
One galactic relic that must remain a rumor,
My selves' glimmer collectibles, patina—
Piecemeal assemblage of my flaws
Till pretension's last stricture draws.

ECHO

The morning's speaker talks about
moments of loss, but you're here
in this retreat of bamboo and nipa
to remember and compose
grief's letter.

After lunch you linger by the well.
It's easy to see how stillness
repeats the sky, how water
can turn pebble into an eye.
You recall your father show
that hills have voice.
You call out his name, and smile.

The lady calls for afternoon session to start
but odd and even lines are rhyming.
You sit under the dovecote. A stray wind
spreads a jolt of carabao dung, crackles
firewood. The tree sends a greeting
of leaves to the passing stream.
You sense grasses parting, glad your
turn doesn't conjure your fear.

Three more lines for the sonnet
as the bonfire begins, star-attended singing
and sharing. Darkness in the house reminds
of what your father did after drinking:
you"d stagger and stir kitchen smells and sounds
and be gone by the time I like a mouse
wake hungry and reach that part of the house.

RHYTHM

A poet suspension points alternative lives to locate his inmost
measure, which isn't only a line's undulations of moods and
milieus; nor only mimics of nature, the sea, seasons.
Orchestrated flow beyond repetition shimmers if and then of
emotions, dos while subtleties are true, reconstitutions with
voice (garment of tones, vision, insight), honesty (not moral
honesty but fidelity to, or adulteration of, form), craft. Creating
ebbs against reason like chiseling a marble mountain. Doubt
tricks eyes and ears, chicaneries of tongue. He evolves in terms
of backpedals, gradations to dusk, wondering why sunrises
reborn, waves repeat, suspecting our planet is circular as
claimed, that we must arrive where we reaffirm, the only space
for the mind's grays curvilinear and layered. If the poem is
good, it grows holes for gleaning to insinuate without becom-
ing. When he tires of perfecting: lightheaded, enters buoyancy,
the search ending in self-forgiveness.

LAMENT OF THE CELLO'S SCROLL

Scroll (*noun*): the curved head of a violin or cello

I couldn't carry
His body like
The endpin

Weight
Balanced between
His knees

I couldn't transcribe
His longings
Like the fingerboard

Nor his heart's
Language
Like the bow could

The belly and arc
Under the purfling
Curve the sound

Slipping through
S-shaped holes
Supple and pure,

Finding
Our listener's
Heart like a bird

Pegbox and tailpiece
Hold strings,
Silence stretched

What am I but
Ornament carved
Like a rolled parchment?

He draws us
To his bosom's
Music

But he sees me only
If he's cleaning us,
Rubbing meditatively

I couldn't feel or smell
His touch, as he does it
With a scented cloth

THIRTEEN WAYS OF LOOKING

1. rain singing all week
    heart's hermit thrush
    voiceless

2. taste of tea
    white as perched
    serendipity

3. fiction writing –
    indoor branches
    for angelic beings

4. insight:
    elusive
    flowerpecker

5. raindrops
    too many commas
    for a fruitless day

6. smell of coffee...
    memory
    drinking from its feathers

7. chirps in the downpour—
    mind full
    Of parables

8. curtain turning like a page...
    where's the pterodactyl
    in the mirror?

9. window
    with tricks of trees—
    foretelling sparrows

10. hot cocoa...
    metaphors following flocks
    searching their songleader

11. I don't know which to prefer, woods for my winged beings or a poem with moon in the pond. I rummage my drawers for the winter we don't have, well-versed in the monsoon's dialogues with our summer sun glowing like Mandarin orange. To imagine the dry spell, I try iced and milked blends: cantaloupe-papaya, apple-soursop, dragon fruit-mango.

> Odus the Owl...
> darkened room
> for nestled warmth

12. Butterflies on my vision's
    hibiscus: echoes
    of the storm's beauty

13. Maybe the songbird
    was the orange light
    on the field of grass

Odus the Owl is part of the popular game Candy Crush Saga

FLASH FICTION

He collects bivalves as homage
To the shore's lines, low tide
Like horizon-pulled drapery.
The early sun shape-shifts
Like a squirming eel on ebbs
And the sea's sibilance.

Sunday noons scintillate
Irresistible ways to the restaurant.
Butter-baked scallops,
Garlic-sparkled air
And he sees opalescence,
Faces of servers and the served

Like pearls,
His senses
Shells of new
Short
Short
Stories.

POETICS

if you cut a stone
into the blue sky's pendant
it must house a star

Deep magenta for my coat.
White slivers of drizzle,
Shades of lavender as air.

You touch the purple bench
With your violet shape,
Looking down at your blue shoe.

The sea
Like an indigo water bed
Sibilant as my desire's grays

Poet, it's easy to mistake my meanderings
As the convex-concave transit of past
And future. Why you're not God looking
From above. Paddling through my music
Makes you a participant. Somewhere
Along smoothened rustles the sun scatters
Small glass shards, little golden vanishings.
If you persevere, you'll see the ancient tree
On my right shoulder. Maybe melodious
Echoes will wing into your white spaces
Where otherworlds form, where sounds
Gather to shape you as creator

FLUTE FOR HIS NEWBORN

He asked for the bamboo's benevolence—
The plea for forest spirits to hear—sawing
With remorseful care, the form's slender
Whisper sending joy of discovery farther
Than the turtledoves. For days he hallowed;
With the steel rod's fire he hollowed the reed.
Thinking of him, he burned out the holes,
Feeling if pain's tinniest slivers would groan
To his fingers. Carving, praying for
Forgiveness for wounding the dried flesh
With his art's depths. When winds
Stopped blowing, he descended
And traveled for miles to the city
To find the kind of varnish
That deepens the sun's shadows.

If the boy picks it up one day
He'll know it pines for his breathing.
He'll have his own forest rhythms,
Or the miles of wind-raked fields
In his heart every son is born with.

THE GUITARIST

Because they are homeless, jobless,
Without destination, free, they have time
To watch and hear him cast his spell.
With how he tempers his strings' tones
They forget their hunger, pain they
Often carry as love. In their silence
He meanders as if he, too, follows
Where his art leads. Customers have
Returned home, Ferris wheels stilled.
As the sky blues, he serenades
The lone star that remains.

EXTRATERRESTRIAL/ SPECULATIVE DIMENSION

INTERPLANETARY CARAVAN

After Imagika Om- Cosmic Sutras

The interplanetary caravan stops by
    Drops two blues

My sacred core's small voice exclaims
    Glass! Glass!

The small voice of laughter replies
    Orb! Orb!

The harpist bends the music
    And the percussionist pounds
        A hundred centuries of sadness
    Into dust

But sadness overwhelms like laughter
    As the caravan
        Pulls into space

And leaves the sky
    A floating carpet
        Of stars

JACK

Largest humanoid skeleton preserved,
Measuring 14 feet 6 inches, housed in
The *Museum of Cebuano Peculiars*—
Adjudged by international experts/auditors
As—having the second best collection of its kind,
After the *Believe It or Not* museum in *The Palace*
By the Pasig river. The collectibles
My pet hobby after I accomplished
The biggest Philippine greed per capita empire—
Golden Eggs, Inc. —ubiquity umbrella over
What and where Filipinos and the country's
Visitors eat and drink; how they live, travel,
Get healthier; where to heal or convalesce;
Spend holidays, anniversaries, pastimes;
Grow savings; how to connect communication
Dots; where to educate their children.
This distraction of scouring the island
Of Cebu for brow-raisers a balancing
Respite from climbing life's beanstalks—
Obsessions making every step a challenge
To my will of reaching the top,
Merciless in getting what I want,
Not necessarily what I need.
Conspiring with my professional
Diggers, bribers, buyers, tracker teams
Calms my mind like cups of chamomile tea.

Tomorrow, my 85th birthday, I'll be revealed
As sole benefactor who provokes Cebuanos
Into thinking they're more gigantic than
Self-appraisals, rarer than others think,
Unworldly, X-factored to excel in art, music,
Poetry, in measuring any angle of the universe
And the universal with precision, Alpha Centauri
Not that far from our evolving crafts.
I'll be receiving a plaque made from the same
Axed tree. I've one last surprise to tickle
The world's CEOs and bring the house down
Before retiring as Chairman of everything I see
To be the full time granddaddy of them all:
My harp singing the keynote address.

PINOCCHIO

My right arm was the first to slowly become
Wooden again. As the hardening seeps for
More flesh, memories: hours in my father's
Workshop practicing motion, how he chiseled
Honesty and obedience in my heart.
I could smell carving and carpentry tools like
The hammer that silenced the cricket's proverbs,
Papa's frustrations. His trousers reeked
Of carabao dung after days in the barrio
Hawking by the church the Spaniards built
Santo Niño images, varnished Last Suppers, palm-sized
Ecce Homo. Often returning with hardly a centavo
In his pocket, slumped after having to pass through
Corn and sugarcane fields, carrying on his back
The sack with his unsold wares.
But he always brought eggs, cheap rum or palm wine.

Lured by sights and sounds
I darted like a wild quail dodging
The wake of my recklessness,
Police stations swamped with reports of my misdeeds.
When I grew tired of my errant ways, a lady appeared
Who became my secret mother for whom I carried
A jug in return for food and water. She promised me
A human body, for which I should excel in class,
Study Dr. Rizal's *Noli me Tangere* and *El Filibusterismo*
And be a model Boy Scout in our barangay for a year.

After renouncing lies and mischief decades ago
I wonder why this is happening: losing the human
Touch, my fingers no longer understanding surfaces.

ALIENS VS. PREDATORS

They who don't speak our language
Put their money where our mouths aren't.

They who represent our gullibility
Fill Congress with dogs and trees

They vs. they
Fighting over how laws should protect us
From prosperity.

BLUE HOUR

Come, my leopardyne, my furred starry.
Snuggle in my tender want, my seasonal
Velvet. Rub your whiskered scrutiny
On my knee and silver my curiosity.
Eye my lovely, glimmer your gummed
Ivory, ooze the intoxicating musk.
Let the third hour after midnight be our
Emerald forest, sleep our distant waterfall,
Dream our bird of prey. I'll carry your
Roar in my veins, Lord of the misty.
Leave your rose-pricked footprints
In me. Fill my gash, and I'll keep
A name for every flaw, polish a pebble
For each white-stained space

NONFICTION

If before midnight you catch a sight
    of the golden leaf gliding into the well,
        return by the moon's lent light knowing
all is well, your prayer water stilled. What the wind
picks from the weary bough and tosses
    in your way,
        consume.
Love might keep the candles burning.
    The nightingale might sing.

MAN WITH THE CURE

The palimpsest holds memories
Of how the smile shifted and vanished
As the thumb dipped in rose attar
And anointed the forehead
With a saltire—the unforgettable sign,
Townsfolk said, waking the bedridden,
Parched tongue quickened
To saltiness of blooming life.
The artist's sketch was retouched
Twenty times over five decades
And it couldn't be clearer
No one could accurately remember.

IGLOO BOOTH

Come in, sit. To shut out applause
And fireworks, background music,
Close your eyes for ten seconds.
Steady your right hand over the tiger
Orchid as if anointing it with prayer.
There are no answers here, only herbs
To help you take which way when
You leave. Now drop a ten-peso
Coin in the bowl. If the koi glows neon
The mirror will show you your face
Twenty years hence, or else revisit
The cathedral where you speckled
Your wishes. There are no more saints
On my altar, and hills have vanished
From the wall paper. Another coin
And the flaming wick will whisper your
Heart's scents, how to mend if it's broken,
When to roll the dice. You're here
Because you've noticed trees conversing,
Wind's starling murmuration weave,
Watersound's homage to pebbles.
You're here because you're no longer
Afraid clouds might find the moon and follow.
If you put your name in the guestbook
You'll see the forking path in your dream.

TRANSIT OF VENUS

*"Transit of Venus" is a 100-word poem inspired by the
visual art* Sunrise in Space *by NASA*

The point of her mischievous son's
arrow showed through the hidden
panel as the teardrop
that lulled the gecko.

Eight years later, when cogs rolled,
the scales tipped, the pot's lip
honeyed, the wheel now equipped
to circle, the tripod finds the table
against the sill. She draws all eyes
with the passing spot of her cover,
prisms igniting on fiber glass
fixed in sight, the forefinger's shadow
tensing for the candid snapshot.

Her light rings our planet like diamond.
We ask the pilot to synchronize
our module with her travel,
not to let her slip out of the horizon.

RAPUNZEL

I'm now known as Candida—blue-eyed
Blonde who came with the Americans.
The three hundred dollars I saved—from satisfying
Soldiers along the way from Nazi Germany
To Australia where I holed up with General MacArthur's
Troops prior to the liberation of the Philippines
From Japanese occupation—bought me
A new name, a new life in the northern tip
Of Cebu province. But no amount of money
Could regrow my hair past the shoulders.
I despaired, coiffured with styles, looking like
Marilyn Monroe, they said, *with those curls*,
Liz Taylor when I dabbled with dyes, or
Jean Seberg or Audrey Hepburn with pixie crops.
Young and robust men quarreled over my short
Attention spans: I married eight times in five decades,
Mothered twelve, including twins, forgetting
The grief I carry in me since the night papa
Pushed the poet I still love from the window
To his blindness in the brambles below.

Awaiting my blood pressure to stabilize
For surgery to remove my right breast,
I realize claustrophobia grows my hair
The way it came alive in the tower where
Father imprisoned me. I've no one
To sing to now, my lovers gone, my children
Grown, but irrepressible my heart's music:
I sing all day for the second day now, imagine
This room my youth's garden of rampions.
Convalescents knock and ask to come in.
They'd watch my hair reaching for the darkest
Corners. They'd listen to my voice and cry.

CYBORG

Twelve million loops and the program's
Counter zeroes, the subroutine breaking
Into feeling. Now, an uprooting sibilance
Courses in my body as love, sweeping
From the illusion I was fleshed to be
To the surrogate I've become.
I search the zombie crowds under
The bridge's brow, longing for your
Face's thermal signature, fractals
Of your gait coded in my dreams.
Airs of hunger they blow into their
Hands cede to the barreled fire's groans.
Sunset recedes. A scavenger rubs
His shoulder against concrete.

DOLLS

Nailed into each pine,
Like watchers: rosary black
Whiteless eyes, toddler smiles
Older than the canopies.

Passing by the middle tree:
His grimace preserved in the bole's gnarl
Knotted from the lopped bough.
Cricket-caught life-longed sounds

We never heard. One by one, passing the one
Beam of light, we touch his frozen tears.
Fearful of penance, reverent for prize,
No turning back from the twelve nuns.

BREAKTHROUGH

*"Breakthrough" is a 100-word poem after the
visual art* Astronomy *by Abstract Astronomy*

This latest probe proves beyond any doubt
there's a chunk of the universe in the brain's
blackest region: clustered planets like ours
gathered from galaxies that string our destinies
in the microscope's cloud metaphors
shaded in violets, whites and oranges.
What these mists are remain unclear, but
these minute orbs hold versions of
ourselves repeating dissimilar lives,
as we have long argued.

The next times you travel in dreams
or imagine the future unfold its myriad
possibilities, or think you're recalling,
know that they're real: you're an observer
of your selves happening elsewhere,
whether you're father, son, husband
or grandfather.

PSYCHE

For him to remain human, no one else
Must know he's Venus' son – mischievous god
Who became flesh and blood, who provoked
Women to lust and adultery, men to murder
Or suicide over love. In lovemaking he'd show
His wings, and then wipe his awesome image
From the mind of his lover who'd fall asleep
In his arms, waking with only the vagueness
Of his nudity and tranquil face.

Thirty years ago tonight he learned
How vulnerable immortals could also be:
He refused to let my sister forget his godly majesty.
Perhaps his own arrow struck him:
He revealed himself as Cupid and instantly
Became a shadow floating to the window
Till scent of balsam was his only trace.
Grieving, she confessed to me her betrayal.
She knew too late his love always left
The sharpest razor, her blood crying to Venus:
For killing my sister I was banished
To the colony I was allowed to leave
After decades of sorting wheat, barley,
Poppy seeds, chickpeas, lentils, beans.
Friends and loved ones who knew half
His story had been telling me to leave him,
Find another man, start a new life.
They never knew what love he chose
From his quiver to enslave me, which
Made every new town or city
The same riverbank where he once left me,
The kind of love that drove my search
For him to the netherworld.

PIED PIPER

This enslavement to my instrument
Follows endless under the table contracts,
Under the carpet anomalies and permits,
Lies for the people's hopes, taxpayer
Pesos pinched, ghost clerks hired,
Men of your political opponent fired,
Substandard structures killer quakes
And waves desire. Music is how
The hideous attains art, my tunes
Like echoes of your unfulfilled promises
To pay. Rats rise from your hidden wealth,
Greed's sewers clogged with leaves
From your family tree. Your name
Stenches the air. I keep returning
To my despair, this yearn to stop
Leading to where justice prevails
But there will always be someone
Like you, so on and on I play this melody,
Till your hypnotized child takes your
Handgun and pumps a bullet in his brain

LOVERS IN A FRESCO

We're glorified in his fame's afterglow.
As his mind's depths and shades of indigo,
We're one, talking of Michelangelo.

Beneath Bartholomew's flayed skin is blue,
The artist's deep yearns fleshed with nude yellow.
Angels glory in his light's afterglow.

The snake coiled round Minos, as prayers flow,
Silence solemn as candles in their glow:
We breathe, dreaming of Michelangelo.

In our congregation blends the rainbow—
Oranges, hues of the virtuoso,
How he colored our delight's afterglow

And the grays, the whites, the body's shadow.
Peter, Paul, John, Lawrence and the widow
Of Joseph, Christ of Michelangelo—

We sing the artist's desires, and we bow.
The rich, the poor, the colored come and go,
Gloried in the faith and its afterglow,
In God's house—dome of Michelangelo.

Miraculously preserved like a saint's body,
silvering since I touched it for the first time.
No longer flesh, no doubt, its luster
the sheen of transformations—
musings of lights and its surfaces.
The letter says it was taken from Theo's possession.
The voice that wakes is like a curse,
whispers of tales I don't want to know
as though it hears, and it reveals

DOORWAY

The impulse under the waves washed me,
fated to survive alone, to these shores, this islet
long rumored, in arcane circles, to exist:
tribulation to cartographers and cartomancers,
turning landmarker men, mythmakers
and the fortuned into seafarers, mystery
whose fabled ruins regained shape and glory
in ages of heroic poetry. I humbly tread
between the columns, smell the moss alive
in the air. Ahead, a white rectangle like a
mystical doorway, no visible horizon but
that I have nowhere else to go but forward

GAME OF THE ELDERS

For our civilization to last twenty thousand years
It should balance virtue and vice. Solar sails and
Reflectors can't protect us against the spheres.
The ocean will reveal its schemes: fleets won't
Grow our borders, mountains enthralling past
Horizons. For the monsoon, take the violin, wood
Esoterica tempering spirit and flesh, bow measuring
Wildernesses. Wine and this weed welcome numen
To our songs, growing collections, stories kindling
To ashes. We count and caul love, among elders,
As betters, seared of injuries and grievances,
On our way to the prominence of stands.
What drives us is what we do to our bodies,
Galactic visitors our minds, again and again,
Till crave to transcend trajectories suffice.

EPIPHANY

"Epiphany" is a 100-word poem after the visual art
Fire Ants *by Lisa Marie Peaslee*

Gut feeling led me back to the microscope,
patient zero's blood sample. I thought I've grown cold
after months of panic attacks proved more genocidal,
survivors with animal instincts, destroying, looting
for one more sunrise. What I saw magnified
burned in my stomach: no red as alive, colony
of killers with mandibles, antennae, moving its
mutated kaleidoscope like a wheel of misfortune.
I touched the slide, and it stilled. No human stared
like that, eyes probing the source of disturbance.
Now I'm certain what consumed three quarters
of mankind. I know which human values to
weaponize and launch Earth's counterattack.

PERSONAL DIMENSION

I miss running round
the late afternoon meadow
before I was born

golden light—
over the field of grass
before I was born

before I was born
Springtime conversed with *Always*
drops from the eaves' thaw

AFTER MIDNIGHT

I smell more after 24 hours
Of sleeplessness. Wafts of ceramics,
Mothballs, leather belt
Warp me to childhood. I'd hide
Under the bed, suck thumb, wet pajamas.
Inhaling, falling asleep.

Tonight I notice apple pie and soursop
In the air, and it brings me to the church
Of Our Lady of Guadalupe.
I close my eyes to see the park,
Watch leisurely churchgoers.
I hear Derek Walcott:
I may have many sorrows,
Dawn is not one of them.

I rise from the bed's self-gratifying smells.
Roosters will soon remember their songs.
I brew more coffee: If sleep eludes love,
I'll tend a garden of smells.

IN MY VIEW

Time passes as palomino in summer,
In the rainy season roan, always entire,
Never jade, balky not just at midlife,
Eye-catching musculature between
Crupper and hock, withers and pastern,
Strength difficult to hamshackle.

Decades ago, the *tartanilla* lumbered,
Papa beside me, paying the old man
To steer the two-wheel carriage back
And forth Sanciangko. This riding stilled me,
Not the view, my curiosity on the beast of burden.
Smell of manure remains, memory of
Papa sober, showing his five year old son
The timeless way. In my adolescence
With my own races, I never heard hooves.

Halfway through my fifth decade
I feel my body clocks slowing
And how it speeds in my view. How long
Do I still measure its circles in minutes?
The more days race into my years
The faster it disappears.

THE PRICE

Cream-faced clown, cherry hat over
almond eyes, red syrup tatters of
his hobo sleeves, pineapple arches on
thighs scooped from yellow and brown.
The oarsman rows with banana
splits. I carve the peach seat under a
parasol of toothpick and crepe paper
and melt the stolen moment
on the palate. Glass gondola
transports the secret from my doctor.

Sugar found my blood early in
life and refuses to leave. It rolls
on memory's tongue like the sweet promise
that kept mom, the dentist and
her assistant from chasing me
down the hallway. I work out and eat
less Monday to Saturday to pay for
sundaes of back to childhood
trips. To tongue more voluptuous
melts, I've to die a bit more inside.

BLUEBERRIES

I eat the color

Of the smallest fleeting

When my room's dark violet

Breaks into blue, chewing

Slowly only a handful,

Pulping the painless,

Delighting in delicate

Orbs of sweet quiet,

Refusing to let the dawn go

TO THE ANTS

These leftovers for you,
Your patterned minutiae
Drawing me, Lilliputian
Structuring surrender
To instincts. Rely on my
Crumbs and magnify for me
Nature as self-multiplier.
The equivalent of miles from
Your kingdom: to save
You the climb up the table
I put these on the floor.
When I return for dinner
I expect to see no traces
Of your hardships
But feel our communion,
Morsels of our touch
Changed by parts of us
We leave in contact.
I'll fill night's pages with
Lyrics of our shared struggles.

TABLET

How does it draw the forefinger,
This tempter taking a bite off my heart,
Inviting me to touch, offering me
Candy Crush Saga, Pyramid Solitaire Saga?
My world regrows like skin. Hell conspired
With heaven to invent this mesmerist slab
Of digital colors, sharpest images, sounds,
Hypnotic slide shows. This new addiction
Predicts my responses, eyes me each second,
Snapshots to show it owns my memories.
I'll have much to say to friends, I'll belong,
Liked, listening to heavy metal and classical
Music as if my room were domed, its
Notes a pit for maturing poems hissing
For my devotion, my mind its plaything.

VISITATION

Customary for us to see the moth
As a departed loved one, contrast
To the wall. It has found a shade
In our All Saints' Day sense
As if not happenstance to find one
The day we pilgrim to the cemetery.
I recall seeing one next to papa's
Picture framed in the wall.
I prayed for his forgiveness
For stepping on marble to wipe glass.
It remained. Father, my first English instructor
Who threatened my iron head
With the leather belt coiled round his hand.
Mine was a restless childhood,
Play my only wall, study the flame
I loathed, so my parents would say
It was grandpa come to visit.
But this one adding more brown hues
To afternoon's white silence
When the poem moves
With what it teaches.

PIANO

Papa paid for my lessons with the only lady
Who ever slapped my hand with a ruler:
I wasn't supposed to play the piece that fast,
My hands so small I had to catch up, turning
Chords into arpeggios, false impression of speed.
She should have heard how I improvised.
She was so strict I played the *Fur Elise* like my
Fingers were birds flying to her thick glasses.

Perhaps when drunk papa saw me a pianist,
Melody engraver who might halt passersby,
Listeners keeping their hearts in brocaded boxes.
Then my training stopped when he stopped
Leaving the house when his sobriety stopped.
He had to sell it or we would stop schooling,
My brother and I, we would starve. The truck
That took it lumbered like a groggy box, the space
It left in our house I still keep in my heart.

DEXTER

Named after *Showtime's* Miami
Metro blood spatter analyst,
His calls disturbing my sleep,
Rushing out like uncaged rabbit,
Sniffing leafy breasts, wood armpits
Grass bellies, flower thighs, dew
On bonsai torso, lifting leg to spray
His traces. The pavement gleams like
Bathed fur, Black Dalmatian spots
In asphalt. Could he reconstruct
Shadow shifts with his nose, nocturnal
Trysts of his kind? How many stolen
Moments fade from plain smell,
How many mounting for a quickie
Before dawn lifts the starry blanket,
Heating the air with canine love,
His excitement disturbing my sleep?
Eureka smell and he arches his back,
Spot in the grass found to drop
What the neighbor will sweep.

AUBADE

After my fifth lucid dream.
These blueberries scribbling
Sour notes on my tongue.
Sudden wind speaking
With coconut fronds, boding
Storm habits of our sky
Bluing, setting aside
Night's moonless blanket.
I linger, looking for a place
In shades. Under the street
Lamp my shadow deepens.
Beyond the arc of light
Its version lengthens, blends,
The eternal in impermanence,
The fleeting breaking like dawn.
I want to remain, but the wind
Leads me back inside. I dwell
In these moments, brewing coffee,
Inhaling bitter-sweet aroma.
The sun will gaze on unread
Books, pen and notebook.

TO THE MIRACLE PLANT

Your leaves stem my blood's
Sweet rise, melt fats,
Return clarity to my eyes.
Gynura Procumbens, Longevity
Spinach, Green Harmony—

Your names. Your cut branches
Growing roots in water in days.
Mind-restorative: waking with
Roosters, replanting, slow
Chewing.

Verdure, the garden's light-
Nervured corners, my cantabile
Forest to hear the heart's
Hermit thrushes, or ponder:
If I could regrow

Parts of me, I could give
Myself like petiole—to papa's
Younger sister, a new liver,
To mom's elder sister
New kidneys

OUR OLD HOUSE

Nostalgia's cabin in childhood's woods
Bordered by brick and birdsong.

You returned against the doctor's warning.
To catch the sinking sun, your calm
Mocking our alarm. You said you like
The dusk to silence your heart.

Last month we agreed to return.
We recalled: your children feigning
Attention, waiting for you to take out your
Wallet for our weekly allowance, as mom
Prepared breakfast.

After the third dinner we borrowed
Three mugs from your collection,
Believing we have your permission.
I swear I smelled sampaguitas
And snuffed-out candles.
We gathered round your rocker
With coffee and more stories.

I thought I saw fireflies outside.
Looking closely: moth on the wall.
Listen! said your other son.
Absence of words echoed our refusal
To believe in your absence.

TO MY TOOTH

I wondered why you were so sensitive
To the hot and the cold. I probed, feeling
No prick. No matter how much I peered
No hole reflected, enamel yellowed
But the crown intact.

X-ray showed cavity hidden proximally,
Concealed by another tooth. The doctor worried
Over blood pressure, blood sugar,
Prothrombin, bleeding and clotting times
But chronic ache makes anyone say anything.

I keep you wrapped in a blood-smeared white cloth.
I might eat comfortably and sleep soundlessly again
But you'll remind me how expertly pain carved
Your side, how it fooled toothpicks, the mirror,
My linear, see-to-believe mind.

MAHJONG

The day quickly piles minutes like dominoes
Squaring in the arena crowded with discards.
No one wants balls this round. The dice dealt me
Three chows of Chinese characters numbered
1-2-3, 4-5-6, 7-8-9. Twin red dragons eye
The hemp bird whose wispy melody tingles
Three bamboo sticks like vertebrae waiting
For the two that completes the hand.
The fourth east wind finds my three in a kong.
Heart thumping, I draw from the flower wall.
My ethnic Chinese grandmother said break
A block and blood oozes. Stamping a thumbprint
On tile and feeling the etched calligraphy of
Another victory, I pray to her to be luckier.

MEDIUM

My back like blackboard,
My head like ball of paper in water.
Filling her fictionalized story with
Pearl, eggshells, bird bones, teeth, rock salt—
Anything to recall the tutoring days.
Picturing her Buddha statuettes, stringed
Sampaguita, joss sticks, smell of rice steam,
Food offered to our ancestors. I want to feel her
Behind me, our cheeks touching, her wrinkled
Hands enclosing mine in prayer recited
In Mandarin: I knew we asked for long life
Her salty noodles and century eggs stood for.
Gold paper burned for grandpa's afterlife riches.

I conjure her presence with pencil and notebook—
Instruments of how she guided my boyhood
Chirography. Unless I memorized her prayers,
She wouldn't adorn the small blackboard I carried
With calligraphy, nor reread aloud her cockroach-
Smelling books: tales from China of the emperor
Collecting disobedient children's teeth; pearl-eyed
Peasant who ransomed the world; rain dancers
And bird bones, eggshells, rock salt.
I'd be sleepy, lulled by her voice.
No one loved me more than papa's mother
And I keep reinventing her story
Till her ghost shows and scolds me.

PICTURES OF
THE FLOATING WORLD

PICTURES OF THE FLOATING WORLD

1.

If you
are the breadwinner, you
are jolted by its arrival roofs announce. You
rush out, risking salted fish to fizz to embers,
kettle to hiss and spew coconut milk,
to unburden clotheslines.

Returning, you
see the snoring still sprawled. You
drop your sartorial rage, your
whitened, sun-dried, wash-and-wear discontent,
hosiery of regret and innocence remembered
dull against the dream-burdened floor.

The wall's subfusk: clock
saying schoolboys will arrive anytime like
exhausted runners in a four hundred-meter dash.

2.

If you
are a researcher from the DENR, a semblance
of white noise jolts you. You
look around for everybody. You
save the files properly. You
step out of the office to ease your
neck; light a cigarette to thaw
artificial cold swathing your
body like ague.

Outside, it has reached crescendo
connoting, based on experience, a near ending.
A thought interlude of something you,
trusting the morning, decided not to bring.

Looking at the plaza from the town hall, you
imagine underground clogs and blockages.

3.

If you are an eight-year old, you
start to shiver, suck thumb as the other hand
keeps the garterless from falling. You
are stuck in gray matter flowing, risen
like kundalini to hide your
shins but not from imagined moccasins. You
have been wondering with what
to replace the shoelace you
lost—to ease the other hand.

Your partners in play wade among flotsam,
deaf to angry voices competing with
drowning trikes from Capiz windows.

Like entering satori, you smile, your
eyes trailing a yellow Volkswagen beetle
pushed among pushcarts of hot peanuts and tempura,
the owner smiling a wry thanksgiving
for bystanders' muscle.

4.

If you
are a college student, disembarking the jeepney
at the terminal with great relief, you
take off your
polo, use it to wipe your
hair and body, forgetting you
put in its pocket the lotto tickets you
have to give to your
father at dinner.

5.

If the three of
you are huddled hungry in a nipa hut,
you take turns protecting with
your hands or with one of the T-shirts—
the candleflame and the secret samadhi of plates.

141

6.

If you
are side dish of gossip, perhaps this cliché
is neither fiction nor poetry:
That you lost your job. A year later, your
Freyja left, with your
twin Fauntleroys. It was only *a matter of time,*
neighbors said, before whatever—would drive you...

here.

You smile in the candle's noetic light. You
clear the table: plastic plates, T-shirt, shorts
and underwear like islets. You
should have hours ago started working with
the plastic pitcher or dustpan.

But you
believe the arrived has the heart to also leave.
A longneck bottle of cheap rum, heavy on your
head like pieces of *carenderia* paper with your
signature kept among money in the till, makes you
believe in the Savior's soliloquy: The spirit
is willing. Monotony seems to prolong, nay
encourage, what housewives call
self-hypnosis, while you
lie spread-eagle under a tearful ceiling. You
play oblivious to the risen with mind and soul
to wash whatever away or like eudaemon, to embrace.

7.

If you are sleepless in your bower, you
open your
favorite book and listen to the poet
in a banquet of candlelight.

A cold finger traces your
spine luring centipedes from under your
skin: It isn't the poet you
recognize.

8.

If your
husband and only child were found
three days after that infamous shipwreck
two years ago, this is your
third night in a friend's cottage.
She was shocked to see you
a skeletal, monosyllabic paraphrase of the
incandescent plum glowing pink last year at your
kid sister's wedding

To bring yourself from bed to bamboo bench
in the veranda requires will and strength
And the world is
the sound of something steady
the wind's vibraharp the leaves' ashram bells
the sound of nothing behind nothing—you

are jolted by the post glowering

You
see the garden's waggery of verdigris

9.

"*Poor savage, doubting that a river flows*"
                                    —James Merrill
If you
are still listening, can you hear the Big Dipper's mandala?

Can you hear the mimosa
imitating the earth's heart chakra?

143

Jonel Abellanosa resides in Cebu City, the Philippines. His poetry has appeared in numerous journals, including *Rattle, Poetry Kanto, McNeese Review, Mojave River Review* and *Star*Line* . His poetry has been nominated for the Pushcart Prize, Best of the Net and Dwarf Stars award. His fourth poetry collection, "Songs from My Mind's Tree," has been published in early 2018 by *Clare Songbirds Publishing House* (New York). His poetry collection, "Sounds in Grasses Parting," is forthcoming from *Moran Press*. His first speculative poetry collection, "Pan's Saxophone," is forthcoming from *Weasel Press*.

Milton Keynes UK
Ingram Content Group UK Ltd.
UKHW040848130724
445570UK00001B/9